**Lin Tidy** was born in  End and left school a education in her twent Joint Honours Degree in I at Nottingham University, ............ .... ... ... had a variety of jobs including barmaid, machinist, shop assistant and primary school teacher.

Lin started writing in 1980 in California after being told that in order to study psychology, it was compulsory to also take the composition class. Encouraged by her lecturer Robert Rippy, Lin continued writing short pieces, reading them to close friends only.

She began writing *The Warrior on the Wall*, her first full-length book, while in prison. Since then an article about her late father titled, *Seven Years in Ireland*, has been published in *Pendulum*, The Journal of MDF the Bipolar Organization.

Lin currently lives in Medway Kent with her dog, Bob.

**(Revised 2014) www.feedaread.com**

# The Warrior on the Wall

Lin Tidy

*To
Fiona,
With thanks
Lin Tidy ♡*

Cover photos by www.area51photography.co.uk

Cover design by Nigel Adams

For my sons, John and Christopher

# Acknowledgements

Where do I start? For all the people, both known to me and unknown, who wrote me hundreds of letters of encouragement during my imprisonment. Each time I was moved from block to block, your love came with me in clear plastic sacks. For my Buddhist family and in particular my mentor, Daisaku Ikeda, whose guidance has taught me to accept responsibility and in doing so, has given me a freedom no one can take away. For Justine and Martin, who cared for Bob as they would their own, taking that one huge worry and lifting it from me. For Watson, who gave me my faith and helped me to understand that value can be created wherever we are. For Flick, always there night and day. For Robbie, who gave me the love story upon which this story clings. For the women of Bronzefield Prison, who had nothing to give but their stories and their friendship. And finally for Maria, the name I have given her in our story. Above and beyond my friend, above and beyond.

'Sorrows come to stretch out  spaces
in the heart for joy'

Edwin Markham

# The Warrior on the Wall

# Preface

When, many years ago, I watched a Palestinian Buddhist and an Israeli Buddhist embrace each other and speak of peace, I knew from that moment that peace, both large and small, was simply just a table and chairs away. I lost this belief for a short while, as though the people around that table had a plate glass sheet between them and the words they spoke were never heard.

Despite all that has happened I continue to believe that it is possible to break through barriers and reach the humanity of the person standing in front of me, those things we all share. That person always wants a better life for their child than theirs. I believe we all share those dark and silent, three o'clock in the morning moments, when all the money, beauty and cleverness in the world just won't stop the fear. And in those moments we need each other.

This book was always intended to be a record, just that, for my family and friends and those who went through this curious time with me. Some of those people were around that table with me, speaking those words, watching them float across the table and fall.

When I think about my Happiness I can hear him in the galley making a healthy lunch with raw vegetables, neatly slicing the turnip I have been leaving on my plate for seventeen years. My Happiness couldn't remember that this is a vegetable I never eat raw. I can feel him in his blue overalls, smeared with diesel, as he stops by the sink in the same galley. And I'd walk over and squeeze his hard, generous chest, made more so by the years of honest work.

'See that vessel,' he'd say, as we looked out across the Washford River from our boat, 'that has a Blackstone in it. I fixed that in 1994 and it's still going.' And he would give me each oiled and rusted detail, each part he'd touched and loved. And I would stop listening, not understanding the compliment he was paying me. But I'd love him for his love of these engines and his pride in the hours he'd worked on them. My Happiness is the best marine engineer in the South West and I'd put my life on him being the best in Britain.

When I think about him, I can hear him playing the same blues riff on his guitar, day after day, as though he was trying to improve on it, hearing something different with each daily note. But to my ears it never changed. It irritated me when he did this;

he knew so many songs and tunes, why continually play that one?

The man who played that blues riff is called Robbie, and today I want to hear that sound as much as I do the voice of my dead mother.

This is not the ending I had written for us. This is not the ending because ours is smiling and golden; smiling as Hess was in the photos Maria sent to me, which arrived the same day that Robbie was arrested. They had been sitting in the marina office at Washford, waiting to be collected along with the rest of our post. In our old and broken boatyard there were no individual post boxes and the posties didn't deliver to our boats. It was dangerous enough for the muddies to walk along green and slimy pontoons, clambering over sharp and splintering boats, walking along narrow edges just a slip away from the oil-filmed water; we wouldn't expect someone else to take that risky journey for us.

*September 25<sup>th</sup> 2009* *The two tall, young detectives talked to us politely. They seemed to take up so much room in our tiny space. I was aware of the shabbiness of our home, a 28ft caravan welded to the top of an old steel boat, a boat I had been converting into a home in my heart for seven years. My dream had been the same as all other boat livers, to travel the world, having adventures, taking my home with me, and like most other boat livers, this dream was never to be realised. But it was one I'd had since a young child*

2

*laying on the Hackney concrete, watching the clouds and wondering where their particular journey would take them. My dream had gradually altered, moving from gypsy caravan to campervan until I finally found the love which had lain undiscovered until I walked down that shaky pontoon in Washford. The smell and touch of boats, the journeys taken and those still to plan with full tanks and cast off ropes, the cramped cosiness for those of us who had chosen to squeeze our lives into their curved walls; in 1992 I found this world and knew I could never leave.*

*When the detectives asked for our laptops I knew something was ending; had I known what it was would I have done something differently that day? I put this question aside, with all of the other unanswerable questions.*

*The large brown envelope on the shelf seemed to be flashing like a beacon and no matter how much I tried I couldn't stop my eyes from going there. Inside it were the photos of Hess which Maria had posted just two days earlier. They showed him playing with the dogs he had come to know, dogs with whom he'd shared his life since I'd stolen him in August 2007. One photo showed him rolling on his back, a supreme gesture of trust, a gesture he'd always shown me since I'd first cared for him. In these photos the sun is shining on his head and he's laughing the way dogs do to let us know that life, at that particular moment, is perfect. I've heard that dogs live in the moment and since I had run away with him, finally coming home only when I had found him a safe place to stay, Hess' life had been a series of perfect moments.*

**March 3<sup>rd</sup> 2009** I've just been given Cell 17, Block 1A in HMP Bronzefield, a Category A, high security prison. My prison number is VM9304. Robbie would tell me later that this is a number I will never forget. Like the phone number of a long dead parent, I would be able to recall it from the hollow in my mind where these things are stored.

Last night I had arrived late as the prison lorry had been stuck in traffic on the M5. I'd seen these lorries go past the courts in Bridgwater and had never really thought about what they might be like inside. Last night I found out that each prisoner is handcuffed to an officer and then placed inside a tiny pod with a blacked out window. The pod was wide enough for my hips, so anyone larger would be squashed against the grey plastic interior. My feet touched the front of the pod. Anyone with larger feet would have to turn those inwards to make them fit. Robbie, with his sweating fear of confined spaces, would have suffered far more than I did, had he taken that long, slow journey.

I'd only ever half glanced at these lorries in the past, with their blackened windows, hiding people of whom I had no knowledge or interest. I now understand that behind each window and in each pod sits a story.

I had an idea, because I was told by Judge Simpton, that I would be here for three months and then released on licence for another three months, during which time I could be sent back to prison if he ordered my arrest. Since then two officers, on two different occasions, have told me that I'll be released earlier. The first officer, at my admission, must have looked inside me and seen my polite, 'please and thank you' fear. She looked at the paper with my June 1$^{st}$ release date and said, 'You'll be out before that.' I now know that she said this for no reason other than kindness. But what I have learned since this all began is to believe nothing I'm told and not to believe that what I know to be true is actually the truth. What I am is the centre of a snowball and the snowball began its roll downhill with my decision to save Hess or perhaps my fear that not making the decision would be something which would later crawl into my mind and occupy it.

I am in here for contempt of court or possibly for breach of a court order; I don't really know because Judge Simpton didn't read out my crime in court. The reason I was in court was because I had been refusing, for twenty months, to return a mongrel dog called Hess, to a woman called Veronica, an ex-actress, who had owned him since her boyfriend walked out and left him with her. In mid-June 2007 Veronica phoned me and asked me to look after him for the night as she had 'done something silly', the something silly being a half-hearted suicide attempt. Veronica sounded coherent and, in her best actress voice, managed to keep my attention. My overriding concern though, perhaps to my shame, perhaps not, was Hess.

Robbie was working on a vessel in the large marina next door where Veronica lived. We had been evicted from there a few months earlier after starting a residents' association, against which the marina owners had put up a valiant battle. We then moved to our current boatyard, a boatyard being a marina without the desire for the title, a sort of Primark version of a designer label. I wanted to stay in the marina and keep fighting, chain our boat to the piles if necessary. I saw our eviction, and our compliance with it, the way I feared the other residents would see it, as defeat and a reason to give up and simply accept the intimidation from the marina owners.

After her phone call I called Robbie and asked him to check on Veronica. He went to her boat and found her on the bed, surrounded by opened bottles of pills and a half empty bottle of wine. Veronica always reminded me of the tragic Blanche DuBois, trying to create a life that ought to be or had been once but no longer was. Robbie talked to her for a while and then returned with Hess. It was a bit of a squeeze in our tiny home and the last thing we needed was an extra dog, particularly one as large as Hess. But as it was only to be temporary, we made room in our home and our lives for him. Seventeen days later Hess was still with us.

Every few days Veronica would call and ask us if we could keep him for another day. I was happy to do this. Then one day she called and asked for him back. I delivered him to her boat. The boat was empty but I left him, feeling uneasy, not knowing where Veronica was or when she would return. I cared for Hess like this until mid-August, with Veronica taking him back for a day or two during this time. With the gift of hindsight I realise that she asked for him back periodically to reinforce the fact that despite his food and vet bills being paid by us, despite the necessity of rearranging my daily life so as not to leave him alone, she was still his owner.

The first time I went out without Hess, leaving him with my dog Bob, I found him waiting on the pontoon for me on my return, tail wagging in that uncertain way a dog has when they're unsure if they're in trouble. He had jumped the gate onto the stern of the boat, walked across the boat next door and climbed the gangway. After that he began to place himself between me and the door so that I was unable to leave without him. He sat by my side constantly, never took his eyes off me, and followed me everywhere I went. The truth of a dog, the head on the knee, need not be questioned or doubted. Sometimes it feels like the only real truth in a world of duplicity.

However, the most noticeable thing Hess did when he fIrst came to us, was to drink copious amounts of water and return to the bowl, staring

7

into it. Those who believe animals have no thought processes other than survival in the here and now, no personalities other than the ones we, their people, design for them, will create another explanation for his behaviour but to us it seemed as though he was checking the bowl to make sure it was full.

I am unable to say everything Veronica did to Hess because the inability to speak is the protection abused animals offer their abusers. I know she left him alone on her boat for days at a time while she stayed with her boyfriend. Hess was often found with no water when Veronica had been gone and someone had heard him howling and eventually gone in to him. Everyone who knew Veronica also knew how to slide the window and reach through to unlock her door. But Hess had also been found without water when Veronica was there and this haunts me more than anything else. I can't think of anything worse than thirst and I can't find any way of explaining how someone could see her dog standing by a dry and dusty bowl and simply walk by. I have no way of explaining or understanding this except to say that Veronica's own drinking began as soon as she got out of bed, often in the early afternoon, and ended when she went to bed in the early hours of the morning. Most of this I only learned after Hess came to stay and a picture of Hess alone and thirsty, while I was just a walk away, is one that comes to me often, at times of happiness, like a cloud across the sun. As a practising Buddhist I am taught and believe that right thought will follow r i g h t  a c t i o n ; take the action and the feeling, the belief, will follow. So I imagine my compassion for Veronica, chant for the compassion and wait to feel it. I wait still.

After the first few days with us, Hess began to let us know things in a way that is again inexplicable and somewhere inside, without being aware, I think I made him a promise. This promise would eventually find me locked in a Bridgewater police cell for nine hours, lead to a seven hour appearance in a magistrates' court, where I was found guilty of theft, two crown court appearances and finally, HMP Bronzefield.

## HMP BRONZEFIELD

In Bronzefield the first two days are induction days. It's a bit like starting a new job except no one says, 'Glad to have you on board.' On the first day we see a doctor and a chaplain. The first doctor I saw explained that he was a local GP who just came in to treat the prisoners; his version of community service perhaps. Around him was an air of superiority, as though the circumstances of our meeting made him a better human being. If he'd been raised by my dad he would know that this isn't the case, that no one is a better human being than me, or the doctor. His questions were ones I'd answered a dozen times in my first two days. Did I use drugs? No. Did I self-harm? No. Did I abuse alcohol? No, unless swearing at a bottle of wine when the cork breaks off counts. The doctor then asked me if I had any health problems. 'Yes,' I told him. 'I have high blood pressure.' I also told him I'd been diagnosed with bipolar disorder 2, not quite as colourful as my dad's bipolar 1, but it was better than nothing. I now call this illness manic depression, since reading 'An Unquiet Mind' and discovering that, just like Kay Bellfield, my mind doesn't live in alternate worlds, one bright orange and balloon-shaped, the other a stone grey crypt. If only this was the case I could simply climb into the crypt, take a pill to put me to sleep and wake when I'm ready to fly into the bright blue again. Since I'd been given this diagnosis it has been used to explain many things to other people but to me it's been of no help. When my mind jumps on a 38 bus to Dalston Junction, having a piece of paper in my hand explaining why I'm on the bus, doesn't stop the journey.

The doctor told me, with a voice as empty as an abandoned warehouse, that this illness wasn't unusual in this place. I think he said this so that I wouldn't feel special but he was too late for that.

He took my blood pressure; it was high. I told him I was on two types of medication for it. He prescribed one. He asked me if I smoked tobacco. The word 'tobacco' seemed a bit redundant as I'd already told him I didn't use drugs. He said it was unusual that I didn't smoke as most women in there did.

'But I won't give you a gold star,' he said.

10

I found out later that due to Health and Safety, my non-smoking status meant that I couldn't share a cell with a smoker.

During my wait to see him a young woman came out from his office, shouting and swearing, in a rage. She was a heroin addict who'd been put on the methadone program, her dosage decided and managed by the prison medical team, a circumstance that must have been a gift to this man. During my time in prison I saw other doctors, including a psychiatrist, but these doctors wore their power comfortably and didn't use it to supplement their unhappy lives. My biggest fear in coming to prison was the thought of violent inmates who would see me as a victim; I believe this is probably the fear of many people who go to prison. But this doctor is the scariest person I have met in here. His violence came in a clean white shirt, a blue polka dot tie and spotless, manicured fingernails.

The kindest person I've met so far is Ellen, a warm Liverpudlian, who helped to process me when I arrived. Ellen was short and muscular, with long straight red hair tied back in a ponytail. She could have been anything from 30 to 50 but I suspect she was at the younger end and her life had aged her. Just as the admissions officer had, Ellen also saw my fear.

'I'm a prisoner like you,' she told me. 'I get out in two weeks and I'm not coming back.'

Ellen was curious and asked why I was in here. I have since learned that this is a question not to ask; if

11

someone wants to say what their crime is, they will, but never ask.

'You don't have to tell me,' she said. Ellen clearly knew the rules but felt safe with this novice, so she broke them. When I told her why I was here she told me that the 'animal ladies' were here too. The 'animal ladies' to whom Ellen referred, were the Huntingdon Life Sciences group, known as SHAC. She said she'd let them know I was here. I couldn't understand why these women might want to know about me. I'd never heard of SHAC but had heard about the 'animal rights' people. As always there was a battle inside me. If we could develop a bomb that could seek out body heat and find its target, could we not find an alternative to animal experimentation? But I had also heard of the campaigners' methods and I just couldn't fit all of those different perspectives into my head. In truth, I was expecting hardened women, women who would not be in the least bit interested in knowing a silly woman doing a few months for a dog.

Last night, my first night, I was placed in the hospital wing. There were two other women in the large grubby room which smelled of tobacco. Four iron beds were lined against the wall and there was a woman on a mattress on the floor. The two women were talking and stopped momentarily as the officer let me in. I chose what appeared to be a vacant bed and put my plastic bag on it, the one in which we put our belongings when we arrive. I

12

didn't know what to do. Should I speak to them, say hello and risk it, the 'it' being something I hadn't yet created? Or should I ignore them and in doing so break another rule?

'Do you mind if I do my evening prayers?' I asked them.

'No, you're alright,' the one in the bed next to me replied. And then I recited the $2^{nd}$ and $16^{th}$ chapter of the Lotus Sutra, performing my first Gongyo in prison in front of a woman who, in that moment, felt like my best friend.

It turned out that she was in prison for a 'mistake' she and her husband had made on their benefit claim form. I also learned that her husband hadn't gone to prison because he'd never been charged, despite signing the fraudulent forms next to her signature.

Lorraine, the woman on the mattress, told me that she was in prison for contempt of court. She had been given 56 days for a civil case and therefore she had to serve her whole sentence. Lorraine was also told that she was unable to receive Legal Aid to fight her case.

When my youngest son Chris, told my grandson Solomon, that I had been put in prison he said, 'I thought only bad people went to prison,' and in a way Solomon understands the system perfectly. The system imprisons bad people, no matter what we've done.

In prison no one tells us what to do. Today I joined the 'downstairs' queue for dinner but I'm an 'upstairs' person. It's all the same queue but the times or rather, our place in the queue, is different. I have just put my canteen list in the 'canteen list' box. A canteen list is a list of items we can buy if we had some money when we came in. As a 'standard' prisoner, all new prisoners are standard, and as a convicted prisoner rather than one on remand, I am allowed to spend £14.00 a week. All toiletries, phone calls, paper, pens, stamps etc. have to come out of this money. Standard prisoners on remand can spend £43.00 a week. Of course money must be in our account in order to spend it. Prisoners work so that money can go into our prison account. I'm not sure how much we earn but possibly enough to cover our £14.00 canteen money. Any money we come in with is automatically put into this account.

My friend Tess has a friend called Lou who is a prison officer. I had a brief conversation with her on the phone prior to my crown court appearance. Lou told me not to worry. 'It's not how you think,' she said, but I wasn't sure how I thought it was. All I knew was fear and all I knew was that my need to keep Hess safe was stronger than my fear. Lou advised me to take some money with me when I went to court. I followed her advice, so my £35 and some c h a n g e automatically went into my prison account. If prisoners come in with no money or are too ill or too old to work, I'm not s u r e w h a t happens when they need toothpaste or credits to use the wing phone booth to call their solicitor or family. Some women are in wheelchairs so I'm not sure how they will get up and down the stairs in the block across the yard to go to work. I don't know how they will earn money to buy the things they need. When I first saw one of the prisoners in a wheelchair it took me by surprise but I suppose even they can commit crimes; they just can't run away.

Over dinner I heard an officer ask a new prisoner if the canteen order she was putting in was her first one. Our first canteen order has to have '1$^{st}$ order' written on it apparently but no one tells us this. I don't know why this is or what will happen to my 1$^{st}$ unmarked, canteen order. No one tells us anything. I have to watch without looking directly at anyone. I have to listen without comment. I have to learn how to live in here. I don't want to ask anyone anything because I'm scared; a wrong word, an emphasis on a syllable, a glance, a smile or non-smile, anything could see me at the end of another prisoner's rage. They can see what I am; I know they can. I stand out no matter how much I try to blend with the paint on the walls. I constantly look for a gentle face or a smile coming my way. In many ways it reminds me of the staffrooms of some of the schools in which I've worked, staffrooms with a chill that could keep meat fresh. Eyes watched me search the cupboard looking for a mug or coffee to use. People spoke with pleated skirt vowels and polished endings but no one spoke to the stranger, the unfortunate supply teacher there for the day, the new teacher who had been told everything about the school, except the most important things, who sits where in the staffroom and why.

As a primary school teacher I was always good at spotting the scared child, new in class, new in school or just scared because life is scary. I could spot this child because this child is me. In Bronzefield there are a rare few who can spot the scared child. Ellen did this and now Faye does this also. Faye is in the next cell to me. Today she said, 'Just ask me if you need to know anything. Don't worry.'

Tonight, my first night on the block, Faye told me to get my flask of hot water before the queue starts. Just before lock up she popped her head around my cell door and threw a small packet on to my bed. The packet contained six biscuits. 'To have with your tea,' she said then she was gone. No smug pat on the back, no sign of self-admiration, just a packet of six round biscuits with a sprinkling of sugar. Faye got me through my first night on the block. In Buddhist terms she is my benefit and I owe her a debt of gratitude. I won't tell her until one of us is leaving because she may not know what she is as it lives in the space inside her.

**March 4**[th] I've just completed my second and final day of induction. I met a young, pretty, well groomed Indian woman who has three young children at home. We swapped stories. She's in for some type of fraud concerning her bank account. She doesn't belong in here either apparently.

'But I do belong in here,' I told her. 'I've broken the law.' She tried to team up with me because she saw us as the same or possibly because she knew I was safe. She has an air of superiority about her and talks about the 'others', young, loud and drug addicted, as though she's better than them. I'm worried for her. I didn't want to listen to what she was saying about them. I like to think that it was because I don't feel superior to the other prisoners but it was probably because I was scared they would hear and beat me senseless or worse still, shout and humiliate me; humiliation and sharks, my two worst fears.

I kept hoping she would stop talking; her voice seemed so loud, even above the shouting that is the normal level of speaking in here. She has been given a release date of mid-April. I'll take that if offered. I can see April. But this is my life for now and I'm not counting on getting out before three months. I'm not counting on anything. I've been counting on things since this all began.

**5:00 pm** A slip of paper has just been silently slipped under my door. I've been given my release date; April 17th 2009. I run next door to tell Faye. Her door is open and she is entertaining other women. I knock politely and she tells me to come in. I show her the paper and I'm laughing. Faye smiles.

'Can they change their mind?' I ask. 'Can they keep me in later than this?'

'No,' she says, 'that's your date, so that's it. That's when you go home.'

The other women in her cell are just looking at me, this strange woman. But they say nothing because they're in Faye's home. They take her lead and smile along with her. Faye is the boss, a kind and benevolent boss.

## HESS

In August 2007, after Hess had been with us for two months, save the occasional day when Veronica asked for him back, Robbie and I decided not to return him. I believe that Robbie, being a farmer's son, didn't have that same desperate, painful need to keep Hess safe, that ability to get inside an animal's skin. This is something I would surrender if I could. I choose to use the word 'ability' rather than 'skill' because I haven't chosen to do it. It doesn't need to be honed or practised. I envy Robbie his ability to help Hess and yet still be able to sleep and smile each time Veronica took him back.

Each time Hess went back for the odd day he seemed to have regressed when he came back to us. Veronica once took him back for a few days and when the call came through to ask if we could have him again, I went to collect him. I could hear him

18

panting as I reached her door, knocking empty bottles flying. I had some difficulty sliding back the window and had to ask a neighbour for help. Opening the door, Hess threw himself at me. I struggled to put on his lead and he dragged me down the pontoon. He didn't need to go to the toilet as he did all of his business on the deck. Some had been there for so long it had turned white and grown fur. Hess seemed to need to get away from the boat as quickly as he could. When I returned to our boat with him he wouldn't stop panting. Robbie laid Hess down and put his hand on his chest. 'His heart's hammering,' he said. It took us two hours of lying next to him, stroking him and talking quietly, before Hess calmed down.

Although my case continued for almost twenty months, my first court appearance was a week after my arrest and ten days after I had found Hess a safe house. The police had been called when I refused to hand Hess over. They visited the office at the marina and took statements from a couple of people. Those who had gone into the boat in response to Hess' howling during Veronica's long absences were not spoken to.

While I was being interviewed under caution by PC Stuart, he said Veronica had informed the police that the RSPCA had visited and confirmed Hess was 'fine'. I asked him if the police would call the RSPCA to check her story. I asked them to do this because I know they hadn't come out. Living in a marina means that

19

nothing happens, particularly a visit from the 'authorities', without everyone knowing. I'm certain that someone at some time would have been concerned enough about Hess to have called the RSPCA. I have also called them on occasions when I have been worried about an animal. I have yet to be successful in getting them to come out. For those who believe that people who wear uniforms automatically do the job that their uniform conveys, the RSPCA is the obvious choice when we see an animal in trouble. It is only when we actually need them that we learn this is often not the case. I have watched programmes about them single-mindedly chasing a swan that has swallowed a fishing hook someone has thoughtlessly left lying around. But trying to get them to come out to the staffie who has been tied up on an eighth floor balcony for two years, getting a kick in the ribs when he barks, is when we learn how 'short staffed' they are and how they have to 'prioritise' their cases.

The police refused to make the call and when I contacted the RSPCA to verify that they hadn't visited Hess, I was told that they were, 'unable to give out this type of information'. This information would have been available to the police and I hoped that if they found out Veronica wasn't telling the truth about the RSPCA then they would be less inclined to see her as a 'victim' and more likely to see that the victim was Hess. But it didn't seem to matter to them. It was then I began to realise that as well as

20

Hess, truth was also a victim in all of this. And if the police weren't interested in it then who would be?

## HMP BRONZEFIELD

**March 4<sup>th</sup>** When I arrived on the block yesterday, a very ordinary middle-aged woman walked into my cell asking for three matches. She could have been anyone's mum and was probably someone's, in her grey cardigan and outdated, shapeless jeans. She wanted to be friendly, with a kind of desperation, and she asked me why I was in prison. I told her. She said she was in for driving while disqualified.

'I only went to the fish shop,' she told me. 'I've never been in prison before.' She looked as lost as I felt. When I asked her what I should do with my canteen order she snatched it out of my hand.

'Come with me,' she said, 'and I'll find out.' She went from cell to cell asking each woman for three matches; she was very specific, three, not four or two. I trailed behind her; after all she was carrying the piece of paper which was the key to a hair wash or a phone call to Robbie. No one was hostile towards her but no one was helpful either. And no one gave her the matches. Then one of the other women sidled up and stood beside me.

'Keep away from her; she's trouble,' she said quietly.

The two cowards in me began a debate. One was saying, 'But it's better to have a friendly face than

21

no one,' while the other was saying, 'Yes, but do you want to be friends with someone who no one likes?' I think coward number two won because I slowly cooled towards her and she went off in search of someone else to be friends with. Now I wonder what sort of 'trouble' she is.

**March 4<sup>th</sup>/5<sup>th</sup> Early hours** I have no clock or watch in my cell so I have no idea what time it is. It is dark, the kind of dark with no stars, that loneliest of times, just before dawn. I can't sleep again and I can't forget the heroin girls crowded into the waiting room yesterday to see the doctor. It was so hard to tell their ages. Some had skin as young and smooth as a child's but when they smiled they had a mouthful of blackened stumps. Their emotions seemed to float just under their skin, ready to burst through. They greeted each other with hugs and kisses, warmth, familiarity. I sat carefully studying the floor with its fresh, dried mop wipes and forgotten corners. I couldn't even study the notice boards for fear of someone thinking I was studying them. But now I can't stop thinking about these women who ought still to be girls; pacing, shouting, swearing, complaining and waiting for their methadone, l i k e  hungry children i n the kitchen. I wonder when they became adult. Once they were like my granddaughter Isla, soft and vulnerable, unknowing. When did this change? Who changed it? Who ripped the wings off the fairies? I can't sleep. Please protect our children.

**March 5<sup>th</sup>** I've just spoken with Robbie. He said that my mum is fine. We decided not to tell her that I was going to court again and would probably go to prison. But now she knows and is worrying about her curtains. I put them in the cleaners for her last week. They were almost stiff with nicotine.

'What about my curtains?' she said to my sister Jean. 'Who will get my curtains? Lin's got the ticket. You can't get them without the ticket.'

If the German bombs couldn't do it, if years of my dad couldn't do it, her youngest daughter in prison definitely won't finish her off. Besides, it's something of a family tradition. My mum's dad served a fortnight in prison for being a bookie's runner. And anyway, the cleaners will give the curtains to my sister; all she has to do is explain what has happened and describe them, red crushed velvet, Mum's winter ones.

There's a beautiful young woman in here, slim, tiny, with pale skin and fine fair hair. Her name is Lizzie. She's pregnant and she's just had a scan, for which she paid a £1 from her canteen money. She came back from the scan and stood at the barred door to the block, smiling, waiting to be let back in. The scan showed that she's expecting a son, after having two girls. We're all so happy for her. Everyone is smiling. I met her when I arrived on Block 1A and she seemed to want to tell me why she was in here. People's stories fascinate me. In or out of prison I need to know where people's lives began, their

23

birthplace, the details that knit a life. Lizzie's story reminds me once again how easy it is to be put in prison; a decision, a non-decision, a thought, an action riding on the back of love or hate.

### LIZZIE

*'I picked up a knife,' she said, almost apologetically. The baby she is expecting is not from the same father as her two daughters. The father of this baby decided to move in with his previous girlfriend. Lizzie was in a rage and went to their flat. She'd been drinking.*

*'I drank and took coke.' There was a kitchen knife lying around. She picked it up. 'I stabbed him in the bum,' Lizzie said, smiling. He went to hospital and had four stitches. He decided not to press charges but the hospital called the police and Lizzie was charged. She told the truth. She was given two years in prison where she'll have her son, in July.*

'That's a lovely time to have a baby,' I said. 'Congratulations. Sons are wonderful.'

**Ms Susan Timmons   died here at Bronzefield on 18<sup>th</sup> September 2005.** There is an on-going investigation, according to the notice board on the landing, just above the turquoise, cushioned armchairs provided for our comfort.

## CHANGING GODS

On page 11 of my 'Rough Guide to Bronzefield' booklet, under 'Faith Centre' it states: *'You can only change your religion by application to the Chaplain.'* I wonder whose permission the Chaplain asks.

**March 5<sup>th</sup> 2:00 pm** The officer has just locked me in my cell because I haven't been given a job yet. Those who don't work get locked in their cells. I've signed up for four jobs, all in the Education block, but I'll take whatever comes along. I don't want them to think I'm difficult. There aren't enough jobs for all the women but we get locked up if we're not working. Many women attend classes in various things. This also counts as work, so they get their wages. The first two days don't count because they were induction days and therefore considered work. So I'm locked in my cell because I haven't been given a job or a course to attend. It isn't punishment; it's simply the system and it doesn't have to be logical.

I have been writing on the b a c k of my police statement because I had no writing pads. My pads have arrived now with my canteen order but I feel that I have to use up all of this statement first, just like I have to eat the cabbage even though I can't wait to get to the roasties. Everything feels so precious.

I haven't had a shower since I first arrived because there are no towels. I keep asking for one but they just don't have any. I can smell myself now so I expect others can smell me too. I'm going to have a shower and use my court clothes to dry myself. I'll have to take my clean clothes to the shower with me as there are no spare dressing gowns.

I have been given prison-issue thick, rough navy blue jogging bottoms, the kind I hate, with the elasticated bottoms, a navy-blue T-shirt, a pair of pyjamas and two pairs of knickers which are too tight. I use one pair with which to wash myself in the morning, running the hot water tap into the vomit patterned stone sink by the door. I have no plug for the sink so it's a case of continuous running water, which strangely bothers me, the thought of wasting hot water.

I'm now counting my days in Twinings Fresh and Fruity teabags. I received a box of 25 last night in my canteen order. I had my first one at 9:00 pm I think. If I have one each night, I'll have my last one on March 28th. Shall I order some more? There have been many mentions of 18 days early release but I don't know if that's 18 days off June 1st or 18 days off April 17th. If it's the latter, that would mean a release date of March 31st, which is three teabag days more than I have teabags. I'll order some more and that'll see me through to April 22nd. Perhaps I'll be sharing the last five on my boat, with Robbie and friends, watching the river and cuddling Bob, my legal dog.

**March 5<sup>th</sup> 3:00 pm** I've just had my cell searched. First I was searched, up and down, back to front, and told to wait outside my cell. I left the door open and watched, feeling very dangerous and hoping that this would give me some kind of acceptance on the wing. My bed was stripped and the seams of the sheets were rubbed between rubber finger and thumb. Everything was removed from my locker: clothes, toiletries. They flipped through the pages of my books, took the lid off my deodorant and shampoo, checked along the top of the thin cotton curtains. The rim of the fixed toilet seat was examined. They left everything out for me to rearrange. Still didn't find the dog though.

I have been told that tomorrow I begin work as a classroom assistant. I had been informed, when I first asked about jobs in the Education block, that they were only open to 'Enhanced' prisoners, so that must be me now; I must be 'Enhanced'; didn't feel a thing. But I couldn't imagine what else I could do in here with any level of competence.

All new prisoners take a maths and english test during induction. We took the tests in the prison library. I sat next to a young Indian woman who appeared to be stuck on a couple of maths questions so I gave her the answers. I was a bit worried that this was against the prison rules but I couldn't watch her struggle with her fractions. I didn't have time to teach her how to work them out. The officers watched me as I showed her my answers

27

but they didn't say anything. Perhaps this will get her a better job in here.

Tomorrow I have an appointment with the Bronzefield Housing Team to see if my home is suitable for HDC, Home Detention Curfew. If I'm given this I will be wearing an electronic tag around my ankle until the end of my sentence in case I sneak out to the Co-Op during the night. Better tell Robbie to get out the vacuum cleaner. I really will be going home on April 17th then.

**March 6th Morning before unlock** Tobacco is the gold in here but for me the gold is ink. I've just bought three pens on my canteen and one doesn't work. I'm really angry. After all, if someone in here bought three pouches of tobacco and one pouch didn't give them lung cancer, how would they feel?

Had a better night's sleep and 'Eureka!' managed to have a poo this morning, the first one since I've been here? My bowels, above everything else, are worrying me. I'm trying to get into a routine now that I'll be working. I worry that I'll be late for work as I have no clock or alarm to wake me up. I need to be up, washed, dressed and finished Gongyo; no relaxing with a cup of tea, chatting to Robbie and looking at our river.

Even though I've broken the law, I hope Nichiren and all the Buddhas will still meet me on Eagle Peak with a nice cup of tea and a giant Eccles Cake.

When I put in my first canteen list I ordered a pair of tweezers. I just don't want sprouting hairs when my visitors come. The hairs may remind Robbie of just how old I really am. During my cell search yesterday, the rather efficient young Asian officer found my tweezers and held them up, as though he'd found a machete. He said something to the young, pretty and rather nervous female officer.

'They're allowed. They're on the canteen,' she said. She appeared to outrank him and he seemed slightly disappointed that I was allowed to keep them. Then the female officer picked up my copy of, 'The Audacity of Hope', and asked me about it. I recommended it but suggested she first read, 'Dreams From My Father'. Mr Efficient then said, 'I think that American election was just a political exercise.'

Hmm. I've never really thought of an election as a political exercise before. That's something to think about, together with who will get us out of our cells if a fire breaks out and this officer happens to be on duty.

## FIRST DAY OF WORK

**March 6th 2:00 pm** I've just completed my first day as a teaching assistant in an ESOL class, working with about ten women from across the globe. The teacher, Iris, appears to have a life that I could eat my dinner off, telling us all several times that both

29

her parents are doctors. My mind put her in a small Oxfordshire village. I gave her a pony called Poppy. Iris' hair is short, neat and shiny and her clothes are clean, informal and kept at the front of her wardrobe for work, not for best. She's round and shortish and wears a belt in her attempt to create or imagine a waist. Iris tried to bring some humour into the class and when she laughed at her own jokes the women smiled politely, not understanding. Iris sat me conspicuously in the front of the blackboard. The women treated me with deference, as though I wasn't a prisoner like them but a teacher like Iris. I wanted to join them at their desks but Iris wanted me at the front.

The women are dignified and quiet. I believe most of them are in prison because of problems with their immigration status but I can't be certain. Perhaps that's just me being a leftie, wanting to create something unjust, something to kick against.

This afternoon I tied back my nicotine-dyed, beige cotton curtains with the two strips of pink J Cloth provided. When I look out from my first floor cell I can see the other blocks. With my block included, they form a square. In the middle of the square are triangular lawns and bare flower beds, save for some newly sprouted, courageous golden and lilac crocuses. It looks like a new council estate, without the special B&Q doors for those who have bought their council house and want the rest of us to know.

30

After lunch I slept so soundly that I didn't hear the officer lock my cell. I woke up when it was unlocked an hour later. Our lunchtime lock up is from 12:45 to 1:45. I have no idea why we're locked in our cells after lunch, perhaps it's to ensure we take our afternoon nap, as genteel young ladies always should. It has a Jane Austen feel about it.

**March 6<sup>th</sup> 3:50pm** I have just returned to my cell from downstairs, where I sat with some of the other women. I skimmed through the wing's copy of The Daily Mail, trying to find who it is I'm supposed to hate today.

Richard Littlejohn was writing of his admiration for the OAPs who have been prosecuted for forgery, having printed thousands of pounds in £20 bank notes. He took up five words to mention that he didn't condone their crime. The rest of the article spoke of his admiration for their fortitude. What would these criminals have to have been in order for him to condemn them; single mothers, immigrants, students, social workers, trade unionists? Our Richard must struggle each day to make all the contradictions in his world fit neatly inside his head.

In today's paper there was also a letter from a woman who was clearly shocked to learn that in this country someone can be arrested and charged with a crime if another person has accused them. She had been made aware of this when her sixty year old sister was arrested and charged because a neighbour had made an accusation that she had damaged a fence.

Opposite me at dinner sat a young black woman, smiling and laughing, perfect t e e t h  a n d neat black hair extensions. I could see her scalp where the plaits had been divided. It was shiny. I think she must have used Vaseline on her hair the way Chris' dad used to, trying to lubricate it into some kind of obedience.

This woman's baby was born on December 27th and she is hoping that he can join her in prison. She was breast feeding him when she was s e n t  here and her milk is still coming through. She has been given three years and will serve eighteen months.

'Why should he be punished while I'm in here,' she said, without a murmur of anger or self- pity. 'My mum says he's fine on Cow & Gate. I started to mix it with my milk to get him used to it because I knew I'd be coming to prison.'
She's hopeful that she can be released early as she's not in for a violent offence.

With my dinner tonight I have a small packet of Diamond crisps (ready salted). The 'best before' date is April 18th 2009. I could take them home with me. It will still be safe to eat them the day after I come out. I wonder if we have a 'best before' date, a time when we're fresh and safe, a date before we begin to complain about the kids scratching our gate with their bikes, a date before we choose Question Time over sex.

Just as it's rude to speak with a mouthful of food, it's also rude to speak with a mouthful of questions. If someone wants to say why they're in prison, they'll find a way of saying it. One overriding feature among the women here is the utter absence of bitterness about their sentences. I have only heard Lorraine complain. Whinging is not attractive and the best thing I can do is to refuse to be a whinger. I feel happy at 5:39 pm and 40 seconds.

**March 6th** I've finally managed to get a pair of white, pseudo Crocs to wear. They feel so wonderful. I'll wash them in my cell sink and then I can wear them without socks. I can now wash the black, sequined, Primark trainers I came in with and wear them when I have a visit. I want to look my best for Robbie.

One of the African women has just collapsed. She was on the wing phone and was given bad news. She's been taken to her cell to recover by some other women. They had their arms across her shoulders and were holding her up. She was wailing.

Today Joyce, one of the other African women, was dancing and shaking her fabulous bottom. She then began to improvise some of the many ways in which a woman can have sex: bored, tired, enthusiastic. Not a swear word or coarse gesture in her whole routine. Classy!

**March 6ᵗʰ 5:30 pm** we've been locked up early today. I think that's the routine for Fridays, Saturdays and Sundays. This is it until morning. The sun is shining and I know the Washford River will be looking beautiful, glowing pink from the gorgeous sunsets we have in the village, courtesy of the pollution from Langage Power Station.

**March 6ᵗʰ Evening** I've just cleaned my cell using a blue J Cloth and Sanex shower cream. After all, it is Friday and I always clean on Friday. Tomorrow night I can turn this week's page over in my diary. There is a river scene on the next page, with an old arched, brick bridge going across. The water looks clean and shallow, the pebbles washed smooth.

**March 7ᵗʰ Morning** They says that early morning waking is a sign of stress. It's the early hours and I'm not stressed. In my head are Judge Simpton's words that at any time during my imprisonment, should I choose to say where Hess is, I can go free. But that's when another sentence would begin for me. How would anyone possibly know if Hess has food or water with Veronica moving to Plymouth, so far away from the boating community who helped him? No, I'll stay where I am. Three more days and March will be in double figures. Saturday. An orangey red day, like the sun. Today I'll stop picking at my left thumb and my right index finger.

I can hear voices and keys. They're unlocking.

Iris, the teacher I worked with yesterday, had a chat with me after class and told me that she's only had this particular class since Tuesday. Then the classroom assistant from next door, a thin, young Romanian woman, brought in a piece of rough A4 paper, folded in half; on it she'd drawn an orange flower and written a few words in English. She looked embarrassed, with the smile of a young girl. Iris also looked uncomfortable at this show of affection, as though she was unused to it. The girl wanted (I'm starting this sentence on one of my new pads. I wonder what day it will be when I finish the last page.) to give Iris something to show she liked her, or felt safe, or wanted to feel safe. It reminded me of the eight year old girls I used to teach. They would draw me pictures and sign them. Sometimes they'd shyly bring them to me, with a silent smile, but often I'd find them on my desk. After a while they'd become lost among the grey lists and world of paperwork that has no room for orange flowers.

There had been a teacher at Oak Green Primary School who drew a white line in front of her desk, across which the children weren't allowed to step. Children would put their pointed toe on the line, testing it. Then they'd pull it back, quickly, as though a crocodile might grab them and pull them under. This method worked well at keeping the children away from the teacher, after all, we don't know what these children are carrying; it may be an orange flower in a rainbow heart.

## CROWN COURT

**March 7**[th] When I went to crown court for my appeal against the Restitution Order, given out at the magistrates' court, I met my first barrister, Miss Shaw, for the first time. I lost the appeal and was ordered once again to return Hess. When I failed to do this I found myself in crown court for a second time and this time my barrister was Trevor Wright. At first, when I said that I wouldn't return Hess, he said coldly, 'Well there's nothing I can do for you then.' Later I was sent down to the cells for two hours, handcuffed to an officer. Judge Simpton wanted to see if I would change my mind. For some reason the officers downstairs in the court left my cell door open. They were very sweet, trying to reassure me that Judge Simpton wasn't that bad. Trevor Wright came down to see me and this time he pleaded with me and said everything he could think of to get me to say where Hess was.

'Save another dog,' he said. 'Get a puppy.' And then he told me that I could be sentenced to two years and I believed him. My heart was pounding. But for some reason it was important to me, not simply that he defended me in court, but that he believed me and wasn't taken in by Veronica.

'Don't worry,' he said, 'she hasn't fooled me. All she needs is her knitting.'

36

I asked him if I might be allowed to read out a statement or if not, that he might be able to read it out for me. Judge Simpton asked to see the statement but it was never read out in court. This is the statement:

### Statement for Court March 2<sup>nd</sup> 2009

*I would like to offer my apologies for my failure to attend court on February 26<sup>th</sup>. The reason for this is that I received no notice of the hearing and indeed, have still not received notice; had I done so I would have attended, as I have on all previous occasions.*

*I understand that if a court orders a defendant to do something, and that order is not obeyed, that the court has to take action otherwise there will be chaos. I understand this.*

*I understand that in the eyes of the law I have committed a crime but I believe that I had no other choice. The people who have witnessed the abuse and neglect of Hess, at the hands of Miss Porter, have never spoken in court, on the advice of my previous solicitor.*

*When Miss Porter handed Hess over to me to care for in June 2007, while she was unwell, I accepted full responsibility to care for and protect him and as it transpired, it was necessary for me to protect him from Miss Porter herself. If there was an animal organisation in this country that I believed would have done this for*

37

*me, I would have turned to them for help. Unfortunately there isn't one, there is only the RSPCA, who I have learned through past experience, do very little to protect and help abused animals until it is often too late and the suffering is extreme.*

*I understand that I could go to prison for refusing to return Hess to Miss Porter. The reason that I am unable to return him is because I believe that her abuse and neglect of him will continue should I do so. I would like the court to know that should I go to prison, when I am freed, my decision will not have changed.*
*Hess is an old dog now and he is finally in a loving home.*

*I would like to thank the court for allowing this statement to be read and I would like to apologise to the taxpayer, of whom I am one, for the cost of this case.*

I believe it was this statement that made Judge Simpton call me 'arrogant'. Although Miss Shaw had advised me earlier to omit the last paragraph, I left it in, believing I had nothing left to lose. Possibly it got me an extra month in here, but who knows.

When Judge Simpton gave me six months I looked up to see Chris smiling. I was puzzled and it was only during our first prison visit I learned that my barrister had also told my son I could receive two years; Chris' smile was one of relief. I mouthed over to him, 'It's alright' and smiled back. Judge

Simpton caught my smile and looked angry, ready to increase my sentence I believed, so I tried to look shaken enough to satisfy him.

Judge Simpton also referred to me as 'highly intelligent' and I wonder why he came to that conclusion, after all I wasn't wearing leather clogs and a hand knitted jumper from the Shetland Isles.

But I also wonder how he decides when someone isn't intelligent and how these opinions affect his sentencing. I believe that his opinion of my intellect did me some harm but now, in the safety of my cell, I feel flattered. Thank you Judge Simpton. Your brief stroking of my ego may have been worth the extra time.

My statement refers to people who have witnessed the abuse and neglect of Hess. However, two people refused to give evidence for their own reasons and I in turn refuse to judge them for this. One of these people had shared a few bottles of wine with Veronica one night and told her of a sexual indiscretion. Afraid that Veronica may remember this and use it against her in some way, she refused to speak in the magistrates' court at my initial trial on July 1st 2008, thirteen months after I had first looked after Hess and eleven months after I had been arrested and charged with his theft. This person had witnessed a drunken Veronica hitting Hess around the head. She also had to ask for water for her own dog during the times she visited Veronica, as there was none down. Hess was screwed up about water for months after he had first come to me. Every time I refilled his bowl I would repeat like a mantra, 'Plenty of water for Hess. Plenty of water for Hess.' It was over a year before he stopped panicking and checking the water bowls. Maria kept three full bowls but still she had to continually top them up as Hess would stand by them until she did. A small drop in the level would cause this behaviour.

The other person who refused to write a statement or speak in court had been Veronica's next door neighbour in the marina. Although not someone who particularly liked dogs, she would go in to Hess when Veronica had been away at her boyfriend's for long periods. Sometimes this was after a phone call from Veronica and sometimes because Hess had been howling for hours. This person would give him food and water and sometimes she would walk him. However, she believed that her mooring would be compromised if she spoke up in court. We'd hoped that in setting up a residents' association we may have helped people feel a little more secure in the marina by giving them a voice. After our eviction and the failure of the residents' association, people just kept their heads down and who could blame them? It seemed that no one could help people who lived on boats, the last group of people in the country to have no protection from summary eviction and harassment. Veronica's neighbour was one of these people. Although she wouldn't provide a statement, I believe that she helped make Hess' life less miserable.

I know some people were angry with these two women for not going to court and speaking up for me but I'm not. They went as far as their courage would take them and I thank them for it. Would I have gone to court for them and risked my mooring or my relationship? I don't know. Besides, Mr Beukes, my second solicitor, said that none of these witnesses were 'material witnesses' as I was being tried for theft, so the treatment of Hess by Veronica was irrelevant.

My advice to anyone who finds themselves in court is this: decide on your priority. If it is to receive a lesser sentence then prostrate yourself to the judge. Don't speak up for yourself or behave as though you are an equal; if you do, expect to be punished for this in addition to your crime.

**March 7th 1:45 pm** the cells have just been unlocked after our post lunch rest. I slept well, on my side, legs bent. I thought of Bob. His favourite place to sleep is in the crook of my legs, on top of the covers or under if he can get away with it. 'A bit of a chancer,' he's been called. He's staying with Justine, Ethan and Martin. Martin lets Bobby sleep on the bed with him and I know they'll look after him as lovingly as they do their own dog, a staffie called Lola. I feel such profound gratitude for what I have; a good man, a weird and wonderful family, steadfast friends and my Buddhist family, all of whom may not understand or agree with my actions but love me anyway.

41

Justine was one of the founder members of the residents' association but had to resign after being threatened. She moved to another marina as soon as a mooring became available.

**March 7th After lock up** This morning Lizzie offered me two stamps. She'd noticed that the two cards I'd posted yesterday were returned to me because they had no stamps on them. I have now discovered that we get two free letters a week. I've sent about five, excluding the cards. At first I refused Lizzie's offer of the stamps but then I changed my mind. I used one for my Visitors Order (VO) and one for mum's Mothers' Day card. That left Ashleigh's birthday card to post. Her birthday is April 4th and she'll be seventeen. There are not enough words in my language to say how proud I am of Ash or how grateful I am that she is a self-contained and happy girl, given all that she's seen and been through.

Later today I asked Lizzie if I could borrow another stamp to post Ashleigh's card. This was a mistake. Lizzie went slightly pink with annoyance and I realised I had crossed a line. To be offered and accept is one thing, to ask is another? She gave me another stamp but I feel some damage has been done and of course I will be worrying endlessly about it. I must return the stamps to her as soon as mine arrive with my canteen.

I had a shower and went to my cell soon after dinner. My hands look spotless, my nails shiny and white. My skin looks pink and healthy. I want to believe that my time in here will eradicate all the bad things I've done, all the times I've hurt my sons or failed them, all the times I've spoken ill of someone because I thought it would make me feel better, waiting for that sense of satisfaction that never arrives, each irritable shout at Bob, each person I've used for my own gain, material or otherwise. I want this time to be a purge for the times I've been curt with my mum or cut short a phone conversation with my brother or sister, for the times I've asked an exhausted Robbie to keep going, to do something for me. For these things I want to believe I'm paying. I want to come out clean and pink and shiny and to be finally able to let go of the past.

Strangely, the action that put me in here is the one thing for which I don't feel I need to pay. Sixteen months after I was arrested I was finally shown a copy of Veronica's statement. This was supposed to have been shown to me before the second hearing so that my solicitor and I could go through it to look for any discrepancies. But the senior partner, who was my original solicitor, quickly handed over my case to Mr Beukes, a solicitor who had recently arrived from South Africa, someone who gave Robbie cause to be concerned about his knowledge and competence in English law. Veronica's statement to the police includes my having said to her, *'You will never see your dog again. I'm rehousing him in London.'* I didn't say this but I believe those few words altered the status of the case to one of theft from one of two slightly strange, middle-aged women, arguing over an elderly mongrel. Had I seen her statement at the beginning we may have been able to contest this.

Veronica's victim statement however was something I was shown quite early on. My first barrister said that one of the problems we had was that Veronica 'presents well'. And as judges are possibly the worst people at judging, someone like Veronica, with her refined and confident voice, would be considered a person of high moral standing by someone who considers the way a person speaks to signify something other than simply the way they speak.

A few weeks after I had been charged with the theft of Hess and had placed him with Maria, I had a doctor's appointment. My doctor's surgery is next door to the village health centre, which is named after the father of one of the owners' of the marina. This family goes back several generations in the village and owns a thousand acres of farmland in Washford, as well as the mooring rights to much of the river. Veronica was also visiting the surgery at the same time, seeing the same doctor in fact. As she came out from her appointment at about 6:00 pm she approached me, smelling of alcohol. I just felt sad and went to give her a cuddle. I have no idea why I did this and I was possibly the last person she would have wanted a cuddle from. But I just looked at her and felt sorry for the life she'd made. Veronica asked me to give back her dog. I replied that this wasn't the place to discuss it but invited her to call me so that we could talk about it. She said she would call but she never did.

We were to learn later that Veronica had developed cancer. She showed up at the first magistrates' court appearance with long, thick dark hair. This turned out to be a wig. Veronica had lost her own lovely hair to chemotherapy.

### KALYX

Bronzefield Prison is run by a company called Kalyx. Their motto is, '**Kalyx - a business with social purpose.**' And who says crime doesn't pay.

On my first induction day I w a s  s e n t  t o the chapel to meet various people and to answer the same set of questions in triplicate. The C h a p l a i n gave me a diary with quotes from the bible on each page. On the inner cover is a yearly calendar that I'm using to mark off the days. It is approximately one inch down and two inches to the left until I can go home.

### ROBBIE

My favourite pages are the middle two where there is a photograph of Tenby Harbour at low tide. I have been looking for a boat that resembles m i n e; there are none. There is a lovely little trawler about forty feet long, navy blue with a white wheelhouse and a red roof. The wheelhouse resembles the one on the William Hunt, the boat Robbie owned when I fell in love with him. Robbie would take the boat out on the late tide and tie up to a buoy in the middle of the river. It always felt to me as though the river belonged to him; he seemed to know it so well. Robbie would play his battered guitar and sing to me. His songs were often about the woman he had once called the love of his life, and his singing of them would make me ache with pain, believing that I would never have his love the way she had. The William Hunt and Robbie became my world and each day that I spent there was a gift to me.

We spent the first five months together in bed, writing, talking, and making love, except for Thursdays when he went to his friend Gary's house to write songs. Under no circumstances was this ever changed. For the first week together we both slept with our clothes on, hardly daring to touch. Many years later Robbie told me he had been so scared of the woman he thought I was. He was in no hurry for sex. But I believed he'd bore of me, this pedestrian, middle-aged woman, seven years his senior. I followed a seven year marriage to his third wife, a woman ten years his junior, so each line of my body was shameful to me, my pot belly a reminder to me of what he could have if he wasn't with me.

Each part of our world seemed to be the life I'd been searching for but didn't know until I had found it. Even the bare metal of the boat walls he had yet to insulate were as they were meant to be. I'd watch the water run down them, the freezing January air being warmed and melted by his wood burner. I'd listen to him chop wood on the iced deck and watch his muscles under his favourite green jumper as he carefully carried the logs down the almost vertical steps into the saloon. Robbie invaded my mind and my heart and I have built my happiness on the foundation of this man, a man who could bake bread, write poetry, a man who could draw out the sorrow of a song with me, his constant and devoted audience, listening, hoping that one day he would feel that way about me. Without him the colour and shape would drain from my life. When I'm no longer on home curfew I'll go with Robbie to Tenby Harbour to find this boat.

## HESS

**March 8th Early hours** I can't sleep again so I'll write some of Hess' story.

He came to us in June 2007, after I received a phone call from Veronica, which was unusual as we didn't call each other. Veronica and I weren't friends, simply acquaintances, usually meeting up at the communal parties attended by the boat dwellers. Robbie had yet to be banned from working in the marina by the marina owners, this was to follow a few months later, after we had formed the residents' association and twenty years after Robbie had first lived and worked in the marina. In reality the owners were unable to prevent Robbie from going about his business so they simply threatened with eviction the owner of any boat he happened to be working on. It seemed as though even our eviction wasn't enough punishment for them; they continued, like someone who had found a dreaded spider, to stamp on us in case we suddenly sprang to life again.

I asked Robbie to check on Veronica, which he did, chatting to her for a while and making sure that she was OK. He then arrived home with Hess.

It was Karen who first noticed that Hess was unable to sit down properly so I booked an appointment with our local vet. Hess was also very constipated and his back was arched. However, after the vet emptied Hess' anal glands, making a point of showing me the jelly-like substance and saying, 'They're very blocked. You can tell because it comes out like jelly,' she then looked in his ears, listened to his heart and wrote, 'All well' on his card. These two words carried huge weight during my case. Had the vet checked, she would have found Hess to be severely dehydrated. But of course this is with hindsight and we have spoken of many 'if onlys' since this time.

Hess stayed with us initially for seventeen days. He drank and drank and began to take on a glow. Eventually his bowels began working properly and he took to leaping like a deer through the marshes along the sea wall. I don't know who was more joyful, Hess leaping or me watching him.

The first time Hess screamed was on the second day with us. I had been sitting for a while, absentmindedly stroking his long ears, when a noise so loud and dreadful came from him. I thought I'd hurt him but he remained where he was and continued to let me stroke his ears. I hadn't hurt him but he was just expecting me to. He did it once more to me during those seventeen days. He also did it twice when Karen was stroking his ears. She was so upset. Hess didn't scream when men were doing it.

Veronica had always m a d e a point o f telling people, 'Don't touch his ears. He d o e s n ' t like it. His previous owners used to pull them.' Hess had been away from his previous owners for seven years, three when he was w i t h T o n y , Veronica's ex-boyfriend, and four with Veronica. For the first three years that he was w i t h her, Veronica didn't leave Hess for days at a time; it was only after she began to see Adam that this happened. After being away from Veronica for a few months Hess learned that no one was going to hurt his ears and he never repeated the behaviour again. I once heard someone say that the worst part of torture is the anticipation.

Veronica promised to reimburse us for food and vet fees. The money never arrived but we didn't care. Hess was safe and loved while he was with us and that was all that mattered. When it appeared as though the police were going to go for a criminal prosecution, I went to the vet and asked for a copy of the bill I had accrued for Hess' treatment, as I may need it in court; they refused to give it to me.

Veronica enjoyed showing people how much control she had over a dog that almost outweighed her. She would order, 'Sit!' in her deep voice, then 'Down!' When Hess was lying down Veronica would shout, 'Chin down!' and Hess would have to put his chin on the floor. He's such a gentle and dignified animal. It was disturbing for me to watch. . . but cruel? Not by any standards that mean anything. Veronica never starved Hess. This would have been evident to neighbours. She would ask people for money for dog food, knowing they would give it because it was for Hess. After a while one particular person stopped giving her money and began giving her dog food instead when she realised that, although Veronica had no money for dog food, she was still getting drunk each day. So by giving dog food instead of money she was also ensuring that she wasn't adding to Veronica's drinking problems. But we had no photos of a skeletal Hess for the RSPCA. No open wounds or burns. Nothing to show. Nothing that would mean anything to a vet, just a dog wounded by a woman whose life had wounded her.

A letter from an RSPCA inspector who responded to the criticism I had given her organisation on the website Robbie set up during this time, confirmed that a vet will never include psychological damage in any report they write. Perhaps they belong to the school that believes a dog is simply an eating and pooing machine and therefore has no psyche to damage.

**March 8<sup>th</sup> Morning. Getting meds** I am receiving my tablet for high blood pressure now. I don't need anything else and feel surprisingly well. While I was in line for my meds, Yvonne, who thinks she may be in until 2015, said she'd received a letter from her mum. It began:

'*I know you don't want to be in prison but I'm glad you are. . . . . . .* ' It ended: '*I'm going on holiday now. I'll send you a postcard.*'

When I woke this morning, having finally fallen asleep as the sky was lightening, seven cards and letters had been pushed under my door. There were many Gosho quotes and guidance from Sensei and my Buddhist friends as well as letters from Robbie, Chris and Katy. Chris had written that I should, '*Look on the bright side; at least you don't have to eat your own cooking.*'

Phyll had written that the Basic Study meeting at her house had been on The Four Debts of Gratitude from volume 1 of the Major Writings of Nichiren Daishonin, so this will be my study for today.

Rosie, a well-spoken young Asian woman, came into my cell today. It's her first time in prison. She's been given six months for fraud. She spoke of the shock to her family that her crime has caused. I told her why I was here and she spoke of her own dog, a Jack Russell cross, who is being cared for by her mum.

(I asked her of course.) He sounds like a typical Jack Russell. Rosie said he'll go after any dog, any size and always fights his corner. Attitude on legs. I like him already.

**March 8th 10:45 am** When I arrived in 1A I was given a pale blue plastic plate and mug, a grey bowl and a spoon, knife and fork of white plastic. Today I am down to a knife only, having misplaced my spoon and fork. I asked at the servery if there were any spares and the officer went to look in the locked cupboard, where she found two spoons. She gave me one. The other she placed in the servery as a spare. I will now guard my cutlery.

We wash our dishes and cutlery in a washing up bowl placed on a table outside the servery. If we arrive slightly late, the water is slimy and lukewarm. We can ask for a fresh bowl from the prisoner who works there but a handful of women are too scared to draw any attention to themselves. I can be found in this group. So sometimes, when I am late getting to the bowl, I wash up in the sink in my cell, safe and alone.

The toilet in my cell has a thick brown build up at the bottom, by the U bend. I am determined to make this disappear before I leave so that the next woman in here doesn't have to see it. Each day I scrub it with my forest-green scourer and hope that I can get another one when this one wears out. The brown build up is getting thinner and lighter; a few more weeks in here and it should be gone.

**March 8ᵗʰ 2:50 pm** I have just woken up after sleeping soundly. I dreamt that someone had phoned and asked if I could re-home their dog. I drove out to their large, rambling house with my sister Jean. Their dog was a strange, small, reddish fluffy thing, like a small Chow. When I sat down he came up to me for a fuss. The middle-aged woman had been crying and I assumed it was because she was losing her dog. I told her that I'd try to find the dog a home. Then a smaller, fawn coloured one appeared and the woman told me that they wanted a home for this dog also. I said I would try. She didn't like the hairs in the house she said. As I was leaving I saw a large man in his thirties. He was sobbing. A young girl of seventeen and a half called Lizzie had died from a bad flu epidemic. I asked the sobbing man when this had happened. It had been thirty-six hours earlier and they were all shocked with grief. The dogs were now an afterthought, a slight nuisance, not mistreated, not neglected. There was just no room in their misery to consider them so they'd decided to have them re-homed. The woman said, 'I can put them in the barn until you come for them.'

'Make sure they have water,' I told her.

'Of course I'll give them water,' she replied, sounding slightly surprised that I would think she might forget.

## LORRAINE

Lorraine, who I met in the hospital wing on my first night, asked me to visit her in her cell today. On the window-ledge were the cartons of milk she had been saving. Her cell was thick with smoke. She told me about her case:

*Lorraine and her husband had bought a piece of land in 1992. It is in rural Lincolnshire and they wanted it for their horses, which they kept on it quite happily for years. In 1996 Lorraine's husband died. In 2001 two houses at the bottom of the track, close to Lorraine's land, came up for sale and were bought by two different people. One of these people is the granddaughter of a local Lincolnshire county councillor. One day Lorraine was approached by this woman who asked her, 'How much do you want for your land?'*

*'Sorry, i t ' s n o t f o r s a l e. My late husband's ashes are buried there,' Lorraine explained.*

*'It will be for sale,' the woman said and walked off, leaving Lorraine slightly puzzled. She had no intention of ever selling her land.*

*Three months later Lorraine received a letter from Lincoln City Council Planning Department telling her that she needed planning permission to keep the horses on her land. Lorraine put in for retrospective planning permission for the stables she'd rebuilt in 2000 and for permission to keep her horses. In 2002 Lorraine was informed that the planning permission had been refused. Two people had complained. The*

54

reason given was that the land was 'agricultural' and horses were not classed as 'livestock'. The woman who wanted Lorraine's land kept horses on her own land, which was also classed as agricultural, despite having stables and not having permission for a 'change of use' from agricultural. Lorraine appealed against the decision and lost her appeal. She was told to remove her stables, horse feeders and internal fences. She was told that the horses could graze but she couldn't bring in food for them, even in the winter. Lorraine went to Lincoln City Council to tell them that swallows were nesting in her stables and as soon as the birds had flown she would remove them.

In 2004 Lorraine was taken to court for refusing to remove the stables. She represented herself as she had no money and, as is often the position in civil cases, was unable to apply for legal aid. In the morning of the court case Lorraine felt it was going well for her. The judge was pleasant and appeared to understand Lorraine's point. She felt that he was supportive of her. Lincoln City Council asked for a break and although reluctant, as the proceedings were almost over, the judge agreed. After lunch the judge's attitude was completely different. He appeared to be confrontational and refused to listen to what Lorraine had to say. The case was adjourned for four months.

When Lorraine went back to court she was allowed to speak for ten minutes. The council spoke for four and a half hours. Lorraine explained that the internal fencing didn't require planning consent and showed the court the information she had acquired to support this. By this time Lorraine had bought some pigs, chickens and goats and the internal fencing was needed to separate the different species. Lorraine explained that the Animal Welfare Act required this. The judge told her to slaughter her animals. Lorraine spoke up for herself.

'According to the Human Rights Act we have a right to enjoy our possessions,' she said.

'You don't have any human rights Mrs Hall. Sit down, replied the judge.

According to Lorraine, Lincoln City Council destroyed the swallows' nest and she wrote to the council letting them know that she was aware of their actions and that she had removed the stables. She then put in planning permission for internal fencing, even though permission wasn't needed. As she had previously paid for this application, according to planning law, she didn't need to pay again. Her application was refused as 'no fee had been paid'. The Lincolnshire Wildlife Trust had written a supporting letter on Lorraine's behalf as the fencing was needed to protect some rare orchids growing on the land.

Lorraine went to court again to show the same judge the information she had downloaded from the internet regarding planning and fees. The judge refused to accept the information. The mobile goat sheds, which Lorraine's sister had put on the land, had to be removed as the judge refused to believe they were mobile, even after being provided with a letter from the manufacturer confirming that they were.

Lorraine began to realise that the more she learned and spoke up for herself, the angrier the judge became.

In 2008 Lorraine was found guilty of disobeying a court order. She removed the fences and her animals grazed together. The shelters were taken down, except for one mobile goat house. The police threatened Lorraine with prosecution. In February 2009 Lorraine found the council removing timber from the dismantled fences and stables. All her chickens were killed by foxes as there was no shelter for them. The council removed everything but Lorraine was told, by the removal company working for the council, that she could claim it all back, which she did. On February 27$^{th}$ 2009 the company showed up to deliver Lorraine's property and she was arrested at her home.

'They weren't police officers. They weren't in uniform and they weren't in a police car. I didn't know who they were,' Lorraine said.

'We're arresting you and taking you to Bronzefield Prison,' they told her.
When she arrived at Bronzefield she was told that she was there for contempt of court.

When I first arrived at Bronzefield I found Lorraine lying on a mattress on the floor in the hospital wing as she has a crumbling spine and was unable to sleep on the bed.

*(Sometime in April she was removed from Bronzefield and sent to another prison. Lorraine was released before serving her full sentence. I went to visit her on my release to hear her story. She has put her land into a trust for her grandchildren. This she feels is the only way to keep it safe. I asked her if she was going to keep fighting.*

*'I can't,' she said.*

*'Perhaps a Human Rights lawyer will be able to help you for nothing,' I suggested. 'You need someone with some influence on your side.'*

*Lorraine took a long drag on her cigarette. She looked exhausted, as thin as a piece of string.*

*'I don't know anyone with influence,' she said.*

*'Perhaps we can work together, do some digging,' I said, instantly remembering my promise to Robbie. Robbie had told me that he didn't want to be involved in any more battles, whether they deserved to be fought or not. I'd promised him that we'd have a quiet life from now on, that I'd have to learn how to keep my head down and keep walking.*

*'I don't want to fight any more,' Lorraine said and I was relieved. I didn't have to break my promise.)*

When I listen to women's stories in here there is a small thought that nuzzles the back of my mind. It is this: 'There must be more to it than that. They wouldn't put you in prison just for that.' And then I smile at the irony in that thought.

**March 8<sup>th</sup> 5:00 pm Lock up** I don't mind lock-up at all. My cell is my world and I feel safer here than anywhere else in prison, and most places out of prison. I have my books, my writing, my Gongyo book. I can create my own life in here. Each day, before final lock up, we can go downstairs and fill our small-stainless steel flask with boiling water then we can make tea in our cells. There's enough for about two cups. I make fruit tea, my warm pink calendar. I've found that if I put one prison-issue black sock inside the other and slide them over the flask, the water stays warm for most of the night.

There are a couple of irritations in here: the electric shock we receive from the cell door whenever we touch it and the mixed-race woman with the cornrows who always seems to want the paper when I'm reading it or wants to sit where I'm sitting. The problem with the door I have rectified by covering my hand with my sleeve before I touch it. The problem with the cornrowed woman will hopefully be resolved once she realizes what a ruthless and menacing person I am, a person not to be messed with.

I'm so glad I no longer smoke. Why did I ever do that? For those who find being controlled difficult, how can they allow their lives to be ruled by these skinny white tyrants? I do miss the company of the smokers' huddle though. They gather in each other's cells, the only place smoking is permitted. Apart from in the cells, Bronzefield operates a 'no-smoking

59

policy, for the Health and Safety of everybody.' I would like to be cynical about this but I'm actually very grateful.

The only problem with early lock up is the length of time between meals, fourteen and a half hours. I get hungry during the night. Women usually squirrel away food in their cell, a biscuit, an apple, a small pouch of cereal. Tonight I have one apple and one orange.

Joyce is the African woman who was dancing. She overheard a conversation I was having with an officer. He was explaining to me that I needed to complete a form in order to ask my family to bring things in, such as clothes and paper. There were no forms available. Joyce said she had a spare. She gave me two. It takes confidence to be kind in here, to approach a stranger. Why am I filled with so much fear?

**March 8<sup>th</sup> Evening** When I saw the first doctor he asked me if I had any dietary requirements. I told him that bread made me ill and badly affected my bowels, so I avoided it. He asked if this was a recommendation from my GP and I told him that it wasn't, just something I had discovered for myself. Because of this he wouldn't allow me to have a wheat free diet. I said, 'That's OK. I'll work around it,' determined as I was by this time to give him no pleasure. After all, I wasn't on heroin, just a wheat free diet. So that's what I'm doing, working around it, avoiding bread, the mainstay of breakfast and the weekend dinners.

On my first induction day I asked the chaplain if she could get back my small transportable mandala or Omomori Gohonzon to give it its correct name. I had taken it to court with me because I knew I'd probably be sent to prison. It was confiscated on my arrival.

**March 8th Night** When I arrived in Bronzefield that night I had to walk along a dimly lit corridor, in the depths of the prison. The officer protectively put up her arm to keep me against the right side of the wall. Along the left wall were cells with small, glassless openings. Once I glanced over and saw a pitch dark face, like a child's. She reached out her arm and called to me. I ignored her.

When I was leaving the hospital wing the next day I again had to walk along this corridor. Someone was throwing food and drink out of the opening. It covered the floor that had been newly cleaned by another prisoner. I realise now that these cells are for the mentally ill, too sick or troublesome to be on the block but too guilty to be in hospital.

I think the sound of a train whistle at night is the loneliest sound in the world.

**March 8<sup>th</sup> Hess** I packed my bag and loaded Hess and Bobby into my car. And I ran. I didn't plan beyond keeping Hess away from Veronica. For three wonderful days we played on the beach while I ignored, 'private number' calls and searched for a place of safety for him. I answered my mobile just once to Veronica. We argued and I accused her of leaving Hess alone for days.

I phoned person after person, looking for a place for him, and was finally given a number to call. Maria answered. When I drove Hess to her home, the area looked grim and rough but the door was answered by someone who looked so out of place. Maria belonged in a Devonshire cottage baking scones.

When I left Hess I knew he was safe. Maria later told me that Hess sat by the door for a long time, waiting for me to come back; not food nor fuss could move him. During Hess' two month stay with us, Robbie was to tell an acquaintance that he hoped Veronica would take Hess back soon as, 'Lin has fallen in love with him'. This statement was to be used time and time again against me, both in our community and in court. It's difficult to explain the full meaning of this because it's true; I had fallen in love with Hess. I'd formed a bond with him and him with me. But to love an animal, or anything else, doesn't mean to have to hold onto it. It means to want it to be safe and loved, by someone else if necessary. Because I loved Hess, and still do, I was able to hand him over to someone else who would also love him.

Robbie and I discussed the possibility of prison but in a way that simply passed the time; neither of us really believed it would happen. We decided that if it should look as though a prison sentence was a possibility, I would be the one to serve the time. Robbie had work and gigs but I was retired, so my time was my own to spend as I wished. I also felt that Robbie wouldn't cope well with prison, but I didn't tell him this.

Strangely, although it was obvious that Robbie was involved in the theft of Hess as much as I was, the police only came after me and the adversaries in our community saved their incriminations and judgments for me only. I was glad of this; Robbie always needed to be liked so much more than I did.

**March 9**[th] **Early hours** I can't sleep again and keep scribbling notes, needing to keep a record of everything that is happening to me. I lay down on the bed and then another idea comes and I jump up to write it down before it goes away. I have been doing this for hours now. One of the other women suggested I speak to the doctor and ask him to give me something. But that would give the doctor a chance to say no and I won't do that. I won't give him any more power over me than he has already. At least while I'm high I'm safely locked in here and can't buy another 40ft concrete yacht that will never go in

63

the water. I wonder where it is now; probably sitting on the hard somewhere posing as someone else's dream.

My light won't switch off but I don't want to tell anyone in case they move me. Cell 17, Block 1A is my home now. I know the people to smile at and speak to and the ones to avert my eyes from. I know where to sit and where not to sit. I know when to fill my flask and when to take my laundry. I know when the showers are empty and which officers are also empty.

My Omomori Gohonzon hasn't arrived. I hope it's safe. Instead I chant to a gouge in the wall. It looks like a Samurai, perhaps Shijo Kingo. His leg is raised as though he's in battle. He looks fearless, like the warrior he was. I'll chant to the warrior on the wall.

Shijo Kingo, like the rest of us, was flawed; a real human being. Nichiren Daishonin gave him guidance, telling him he should he stay at home when he's drinking sake. But if he was around today he'd be the man we could rely on, the constant friend, the one we call, the one who would say, 'I'll be there in five minutes,' and arrive in three, wheels screeching.

**March 9th 11:05 am** I've been called out of work to move to Block 3A. I'm scared. But when I get back to my cell I find that the lovely Ellie is being moved with me and she keeps me calm.

'Don't worry,' she says, 'I think we're going to the same block.'

Ellie has been friendly and kind since I first met her. Sometimes I've been in her cell for a chat, sitting on her bed watching her roll ciggies. She doesn't have that hardened manner, just the air of someone who has accepted the life she has, just as she accepted the sentence she's been given for shoplifting clothes to give to her friends and family, feeding her addiction to kindness. Ellie is one of our gentle people.

I've been given Cell 17 again. Ellie is next door in Cell 18. If there was a garden fence we could talk over it, swapping plant cuttings, our hands covered in soil.

Again I have to wait for a towel as there's a shortage. I was told by the officer, a tall, no nonsense black woman with orange cropped hair that I would have to sign up for a dressing gown and wait my turn. Is that a turn to be given one or a turn to wear one?

**March 9th After lock up** The officer, Beverley, runs a tight ship. Firm but fair I believe is the adage. But I like her because she makes me feel safe; she watches for the queue jumpers and jumps on them in turn. It's not the having to wait a few minutes longer for our food that makes the queue jumpers dangerous but the silence with which they're met. The silence tells them just what they can get away with in here, who they can bully and steal from, while the officers studiously stand and re-read the notices they have read a hundred times.

I'll begin evening Gongyo soon. There's no warrior on the wall here. 'Julie loves Wiggy 4 ever' isn't quite the same but who am I to say that Julie and Wiggy aren't as brave and noble as Shigo Kingo.

Today Ellie asked me what a Buddhist is and I told her about her Buddhahood.

'That's what we have Ellie, you, me, everyone.' I didn't even make my, 'But not Margaret Thatcher,' joke. I didn't want anything to blemish the moment when Ellie found out that she has Buddhahood. She's waited too long.

'I want a different life now. I don't want to come to prison again,' she said.

Ellie will be released on March 20th 2009 and she's made a calendar on her wall with squares of paper. I want to teach her to chant before she reaches that last square.

Today Iris was off sick so Joe took her class. I was called away to move and went back after lunch but there was no lesson. I sat in on Joe's French class. I can now say, 'Sorry but it is not possible for me to do it like that,' in French. Should come in handy the next time Robbie and I are having sex.

Beverley bought me in a card from Jilly with this month's study. It's from 'The Dragon Gate' and it will be my study for tonight.

Someone has inadvertently given me a TV in my cell, even though I haven't paid for it. This will test my resolve. Robbie would be very disappointed in me if he knew I was watching telly in here; he would want me to be doing something constructive. Sometimes, when I hear his big footsteps coming onto the boat, I quickly turn off it off so he doesn't know I've been watching it. At home our little telly is in our tiny cabin, sitting on a shelf over the bed. Robbie built both the bed and the shelf. The telly has a bungee strap around it in case we have rough weather. It once fell on us during the night so bungee straps are a must-have on boats. I spend a lot of time in the cabin as it's the only place I can be alone, except for Bob that is, but he's a man of few words. We always seem to have guests. Robbie likes company; he's very sociable and can talk for hours. He hasn't quite learned the social rules of conversation, so he tends to take over, not reading the body language. But Robbie can talk about anything, from the history of carrier bags to the design of teapot spouts in post-war Britain. That may be a slight exaggeration; he does tell me I have a habit of doing this. But what I envy is his ability to talk to anyone and welcome people at any time of the day or night. I wish I had a heart that big and generous.

**March 10**[th] March is in double figures and I slept. There's a woman in Block 3A who has a broken hand. She had a fight with a woman she called a 'black bastard'. She's now being bullied for being a racist by a group of young white girls who speak in black street English.

This evening Ellie shyly asked me if she could use my Alberta Balsam shampoo. She's been dropping hints all day but I hadn't realised. Then I said, 'Why don't you use it the night before you're released.' She looked pleased. But Ellie wanted to use it right then and I felt ashamed that I hadn't offered it, trying to conserve it for a while longer. Eleven days is a lifetime in here. I gave her the shampoo and conditioner. When she took it she made me a promise.

'I won't use too much,' she said. When she returned it, hardly any had been used. She kept her promise. I feel so guilty. I have so much. I'm going to order her a bottle of shampoo and conditioner on my canteen, Sunkiss Raspberry flavour. I want her to feel special.

When I went to work today Iris was back and in a foul mood. She's covered in a rash that looks stress related. When I began work last Friday she spoke to me of the importance of meeting targets in the ESOL class. Today she asked me to sit with the students, which is where I had always wanted to sit; after all I'm searched when I leave the room, just as all the other prisoners are. She seemed angry about something. There was a chill about her.

I had an appointment today with the prison version of Job Centre Plus. I was told that my state pension has been stopped while I'm in here but they're unable to stop my teachers' pension as it's a private one. I hope this annoys them, whoever they are.


**March 10<sup>th</sup> After lunch** I've now realised that the reason I couldn't sleep, with words and ideas needing to be written down every few minutes, was because I was high. Now I can sleep but I have started to drag memories out of the shadows and I cry with my door closed. I don't want anyone to see me. Crying isn't seen as a sign of weakness in here. It just means that another prisoner will try to make it better and then wander away, believing they have.

Ellie lost her temper in the IT class today and will be punished, possibly downgraded to 'Basic'. I had a chat with her later and told her, 'Don't give them your power Ellie. You have Buddhahood. If you feel as though you're losing it just tell yourself, "No, I have Buddhahood. I'm in control of my life."'

I then told her how grateful I was to her.

'You're a good person Ellie. You don't know how much you've helped me. You didn't have to but you did. You made a difference.'

Ellie began crying. We both did. She said, 'This is the first time I've cried since I've been here. I know I'm a good person but people don't tell me. No one has ever told me.'

I told her that I'd teach her to chant Nam Myoho Renge Kyo, to support her in the new life she's determined to have. Ellie is my benefit, one of many in Bronzefield. Tomorrow I will teach her to chant.

69

**March 10<sup>th</sup> After lock up** I have succumbed to TV and just watched a programme about Whipps Cross Hospital, a place that bought Chris into the world and John, my first born, back into the sober world, where we greeted him like a soldier we believed we had lost on the battlefield.

**March 11<sup>th</sup> Before unlock** Another night's sleep. The morning sounds in prison begin long before they unlock our cells. A lone call, a cell opening for someone who has an early job or a court date, the sound of keys rattling, always the keys. At first they were a constant reminder of where I am. Now? They're simply part of my life. My outside manners have become more polished in here, more please and thank you. Am I trying to separate myself, let people know I'm not really 'prison material' as Leah said in her letter? Or am I just trying to hold onto myself?

**Prison Courtesy** If a ravaged, toothless woman accidentally brushes up against another ravaged toothless woman, it usually goes like this:

'Sorry darling.'

'That's alright darling.'

There is more courtesy on the wing between prisoners, than there is on the Education block between Iris and the students. The perfect life is rude to the imperfect lives, with that air of good walking shoes and stripped pine book shelves.

Joe is different; young, kind and slightly too uncomfortable with his role to raise his voice at the women. He has been brought up well, a 'nice' man. Yesterday I asked him if he could teach me to say, 'It's a fair cop guv,' in French. He smiled. I told him why I was in prison but I don't think he believed me. I don't know why I told him really, perhaps to make it real, perhaps to try to elevate myself in his eyes. Prefer the first reason so I'll keep that one.

I'm a proper prisoner now. I've taken one of my shoelaces and hung my ID card on it. I wear it around my neck. It's official; I belong here.

**March 11<sup>th</sup> After lock up** I still can't get used to being patted down when I leave the classroom. Today one of the English women in the classroom along the corridor, tried to sneak out a piece of A4 coloured paper in her folder. The officer took it off her, holding it up as though she'd found something dangerous. It seemed so petty, such a small, petty cruelty and it's the small cruelties that get to me. I wonder what she was going to do with it; make a card to send to her children, a picture to brighten her cell?

Yesterday in French class Dorothy, a well-spoken, educated black woman, asked Joe why no certificates were given out for French, as they were for all the other courses. Joe explained that because people are so transient in the prison population, there was really no beginning or end to the course. But Dorothy wouldn't give up until Joe agreed to make up a certificate for his students. She ended her haranguing of him by saying, 'It's not for me Joe. I have my qualifications. It's for the women in here who have nothing. It's something they can have, something they've achieved.'

I went to French class today and was told that Dorothy has been sent to another prison. I miss her. People are removed from wings, blocks and Bronzefield suddenly, no time to say goodbye or return a borrowed item.

Iris' rash was a bit better today. The red flecks had climbed up from her neck and were huddled together around her chin. Today Iris was asking each woman to speak a sentence in English. The sentence had to contain some particular words. When it came to Lien, a shy Chinese woman, she began to cry. Her sentence was, 'I have big problem in this prison.' Iris tried to be kind but was only able to keep it up for a minute as Lien was holding up the lesson. When we had our usual morning break, to drink our weak orange squash and look out of the window, I found a young woman wearing a purple sweatshirt. Purple sweatshirts have a job in Bronzefield, so I told her about Lien and how worried I was about her. The young woman's name was Kat, which is probably short for Katherine. She is a Listener, signified by the purple sweatshirts. Kat is going to talk to her. I think Lien is worried about her immigration status. There is 'immigration' in the abstract, the Daily Mail type, people we don't meet and aren't likely to. And there is Lien, a quiet, scared woman, crying quietly because she is embarrassed by her tears and knows how 'we' feel about her and other immigrants.

When a woman leaves prison we're all happy for her, no matter if we've spoken to her or not. She's going to choose her food, laugh with her friends, help her children with their homework, and hug her man. Until we're able to do these things for ourselves, she'll do them all for us.

This morning during breakfast, R Kelly came on the radio singing, 'I Believe I Can Fly.' One by one women began joining in. Young women, criminals, drug addicted, scarred, they all sang out, 'I believe I can fly. I believe I can touch the sky.' They sang as though they believed they could and no one could stop them. I really hope they can. Fly my wonderful women.

Tonight I taught Ellie to chant. Tomorrow I will ask her if she wants to chant with me.

Yvonne, who received the letter from her mum, is in prison for the twenty-ninth time. I have no idea how old she is but possibly in her thirties. This time she's in because she stabbed her boyfriend again. Yvonne's violence is palpable. I think she could have a fight in an empty house.


**March 12<sup>th</sup> Before unlock** As soon as the door is unlocked we have to be up and dressed, ready for breakfast and our medication. The trick for me is that as soon as I wake up, I wash at the stone sink by the door. I listen for an officer approaching to make sure that I won't be caught in the act. Top first, quickly, using my knickers as a flannel, then deodorant, bra, T-shirt. The bottom next. My fear is that I'll be standing eighteen inches from the door, semi-naked, when the officer comes to open it.

The toilet is next to the sink, about three feet from the door. When the door is shut the toilet can only be seen through the vertical, 12in by 4in opening and then only by a determined officer standing by the side and turning his eyes to the right.

**March 12<sup>th</sup> Breakfast** This morning, when I went down for breakfast, two or three women said, 'Morning Lin,' and it felt good, as though I belonged, as though I'd made friends.

When I arrived in 3A, Manisha was here. This was the young Indian woman I'd met on my induction. Last night she asked me to write a letter to her employer asking them to keep her job open for her. A change has come over Manisha in the nine days since I first met her. She, like me, is losing her fear. Manisha has also teamed up with someone she would probably never spend any time with on the outside. We look for companionship, a cushion between us and prison, someone to learn with and from, familiarity with a routine with which they may have had only twenty-four hours more experience.

**March 12<sup>th</sup> After lunch lock up** I've just had a morning in class. I started chatting to Adriana, a Romanian woman who lived and worked in Spain for ten years. She told me about her dogs and cats in East Ham. Her descriptions were lovely and all the more so for the fractured English. Adriana told me that she is unable to have children so her animals are her family. Her husband is caring for them. (I asked!) She has no idea how long she'll be in prison

**Present Continuous** Today Iris taught the Present Continuous or should that be, 'is teaching the Present Continuous'? She asked me to compile a list of actions and then sent me to wait outside the door. Each woman was then asked to come out to me so that I could give them an action to mime in the classroom for the others to guess. On my list I had: eating an ice cream, skipping, playing tennis, cleaning a window etc. There was an action for everyone. When the young, pregnant Muslim woman came out Iris wanted her to mime 'having a baby'. That wasn't on my list. The woman looked confused and politely declined, accepting my suggestion of 'drawing a picture' instead. I don't know what was in Iris' head when she suggested the mime but somewhere, during her wicker-basket and fresh eggs childhood, she wasn't taught that the definition of 'class' is the art of making someone feel comfortable.

**March 12th between dinner and lock up** I've just chanted with Ellie in her cell and perhaps that's the reason I'm here; Hess was the means to this end.

Manisha is distraught. She's just been told that she's being moved to Morton Hall Prison in Lincoln because that's where 'foreign nationals' are sent. Manisha has been in the United Kingdom for fifteen years and has a British passport. I'll chant for her tonight.

Once or twice Iris has spoken to me of the disappointment and surprise she feels at the lack of progress made by the women in her class.

'They should know all this!' she says, while the women juggle with the 'do' and 'does' in their sentences. 'They've been learning English for six weeks! They should know this!'

I feel uncomfortable when she does this, when she demeans their achievements, as though 'they're' somehow lacking and I belong in her special 'clever' club. She asked me once what qualifications I have: a BA Hons, a PGCE and a criminal record actually Iris.

**March 12th 8:00 pm** From that day in August 2007 when I left with Hess, people have told me to lie. 'Just say you took him for a walk and he went off after a rabbit,' was the most frequent suggestion. I got the impression that even the police hoped I would lie. But the truth is the only tangible thing I've had to cling to. To throw in a lie would be like peeing in the soup; even if I couldn't taste it, I would know it was there. It became more than simply keeping Hess safe I began to understand. If I could keep it all in a straight line, it would be one straight and true thing, one thing I could keep with me, look at and rely on.

Since Manisha received her notice to move I have realised that I can't assume I'm at Bronzefield until my release. I could be moved the day before my release if the cogs in the system line up that way.

For years I've woken each morning with dread in the pit of my stomach, a nameless fear. Each day, for years, I want to stay in the safety of my bed, afraid of what is waiting for me on this day. And each day I get up and begin. Since I've been in HMP Bronzefield this waking up fear has stopped.

**March 13th Early hours**   Friday the 13th. Oh hell! I'd better not go out today; I may accidentally walk under the ladder leaning up against the prison wall.

Not sleeping again.

### SECOND HEARING AT BRIDGEWATER MAGISTRATES' COURT. July 1st 2008

Initially I had been given Mr Sharp as my solicitor, a senior partner in a local Washford practice. When I told him that I felt I had no choice but to plead guilty he advised me to plead not guilty. I followed his advice. The next time I phoned his office I was told that Mr Sharp was no longer acting for me and that Mr Beukes was now my solicitor. Mr Beukes is a South African solicitor and appeared to be rather unfamiliar with British law. During my hearing for theft at the magistrates' court, Mr Beukes announced to the court that they had no powers to make me return Hess. The clerk of the court then left the room and returned with several books. Mr Adams, the senior prosecutor who'd been assigned to my case, along with the clerk of the court, pored over these for a while and finally came up with a restitution order. I was given an eighteen month conditional discharge, court costs and twenty-eight days to return Hess. Mr Beukes advised me not to appeal but I knew only two things: firstly, I would never return Hess and secondly, in twenty-nine days I would be in breach of a court order. The trial began at 10 am and ended at 5:20 pm.

Definition of theft was discussed in the court and they searched for a precedent, finally coming up with that of 'Rostron and Collinson 2003'. This case involved two men who, wearing wetsuits, regularly trespassed onto a golf course so they could go into the lake to collect the lost golf balls. The case received a lot of publicity at the time, particularly when one defendant was sentenced to prison. He appealed and was given a community penalty. These two men were running a business and making several thousand pounds annually. Mr Beukes did make the point that theft usually involves some type of gain on the part of the thief. In my case, as well as paying for

78

all of Hess' upkeep, the market value of Hess, according to the court, was zero. But in order to proceed with a criminal case against me a precedent was needed and this was the closest they could find.

We had taken Hess to April Mason, a well-regarded dog behaviourist, who had written a report on her observations of Hess' behaviour, stating that in her opinion Hess behaved like an abused dog. She said that for a dog to exhibit fearful behaviour, as Hess did about water and having his ears touched, the cause of this behaviour had to have been something that the dog experienced many times and even when the cause had stopped, it was still possible for the dog to elicit that behaviour if reminded of the abuse. The report was brushed aside by the prosecutor, who said that Hess had been seen by April Mason several months after he had left Veronica, the implication being that the abuse April believed had happened was either committed by me or the person with whom I had placed him. Even Mr Adams, the prosecutor, agreed that this was unlikely. Mr Beukes remained silent.

During the lunch break I went with some friends to the court cafe, as did Mr Adams. While in the cafe some solicitors came in and began to make jokes at Mr Adams' expense.

'We're going to send all the dog cases to him from now on,' they joked. Mr Adams joined in the banter.

'How many dog cases have you had?' I piped up.

'Just this one,' they replied, 'but I think we had a badger case a few years ago.'

**March 13<sup>th</sup> After lunch lock up** On my plate I always leave the best until last. In my wardrobe are many 'special occasion' clothes, just simple things, 'best' jeans, a long inexpensive dress saved for that summer party. I have decided that when I'm freed I'll stop this habit. Things change so quickly in here; people arrive, people leave, no time to say anything except 'good luck,' as we pass in the wing, carrying our belongings. I won't wait for the special occasion again; it may pass me by, carried away in a clear plastic sack.

### LIEN

*Today Lien was still worrying. She was told that she had been given an 18 day early release and may be leaving at any time. At 10:50 am an officer came into the classroom and announced to her, 'You're leaving.' We just burst into spontaneous applause, even Joe. I have found out that Lien is in prison for selling DVDs on the street. Two months ago she was mugged and bitten by the dog the mugger was using as a weapon. Lien was too afraid to go to the police or the hospital.*

### KHADRA

*The name of the pregnant Muslim woman is Khadra and she's from Somalia. Her baby I learned, by actions and counting fingers, will be an autumn baby.*

*Khadra, like me, has been given an HDC date but she doesn't know how to apply for it. No one has explained to her that she doesn't have to.*

*She asked me to look at her immigration papers. Khadra fears that she'll be sent back to Somalia, a country she left when she was eight. She moved to Saudi Arabia with her family to escape the war. Khadra told me that Somalian women are used as slaves in Saudi Arabia. A life of servitude waits for them. Khadra's husband is in London and can apply for a British passport but hasn't. I advised her to urge him to apply and then their baby will be a British Citizen I think. Khadra was caught crossing from France to England to join her husband. Joe told her that the British Government didn't usually send people back to Somalia. He took the time to explain this, breaking off the lesson in 'shopping' to sit with her.*

*Joe doesn't seem too concerned about ESOL targets, preferring to spend the time helping a terrified, pregnant woman. If he's hoping for promotion in this place, this isn't the way to get it.*

**March 13<sup>th</sup> After lunch, free afternoon** I've just been to see the doctor again, the shrink this time. Not Teflon-coated but a real person. We chatted. She asked me how my mental state was. I'm not sure if I'm the right person to assess that.

# BADRIA

Badria is about eighteen and an Afghan Hindu. Hindus are often faced with persecution in Afghanistan. I was introduced to her by Manisha. Badria was explaining that the officers in the Afghanistan army are ex-Taliban. In order to move around or go to the temple, her father had to pay at each checkpoint. Badria and her younger sister and mother rarely left the house but army officers began to visit. They told her father that if he didn't pay them money they would rape his wife and daughters. So he paid. The soldiers kept returning and her father kept paying to keep his family safe.

The family made a decision to find an agent to get them out of the country but they discovered that they didn't have enough money left for the whole family. Badria explained that her father decided to stay behind in order that his wife and daughters could leave, because in Afghanistan a family with no male head wouldn't survive. Badria said that they have no idea where her father is, or he them. An agent doesn't tell the family where they are going, often because he is just the first link in the chain.

When the family arrived in England they met the immigration service. Badria said, 'We left Afghanistan because it's dangerous. My mother is very ill and my sister was disabled in a bomb blast. We thought we were safe and then we met the immigration.'

The officials began asking Badria's mother questions about Hinduism. Her mother was unable to answer so the immigration decided that the family was Muslim. Badria asked immigration to ask her and her sister the questions as their mother never went out and was virtually cut off from the world. Badria and her sister were able to answer the questions about their faith. The officials then decided that Badria's mother was lying and that she wasn't really their mother. When Badria offered to take a DNA test the officials changed their mind. The family settled and Badria began college, studying Law and Business.

Last Saturday immigration showed up at their home. They want to deport the family but are investigating their 'status'. While the investigation is on-going, immigration has decided to hold Badria in prison to stop the family from going into hiding. Badria said,

'My teachers will be wondering where I am. I never miss class.'

**March 13<sup>th</sup> After lock up** Tonight I miss my dad and wonder what he would say to me. I know I could explain this to him and he'd understand. He turned his head away from me when I went to see him in the hospital. I couldn't save him; I'd let him down and this is how he told me. I watched them killing him and didn't know it was happening. He was struggling to breathe and kept taking off his oxygen mask to talk to me. I don't know what he was trying to say to me and the nurse kept putting the mask back on him.

The next time I saw him he was spread-eagled on a bed while the HDU doctors fought to save him. Too late. They tortured him for another two weeks until it was time for the decision. The 'yeses' went from Mum to Jean to John. I ended my dad's life with a nod. I watched the tears trickle out of the corner of his eyes. The nurse said that this is normal but I knew better. It was Dad saying goodbye to a life he wanted to hold onto. He wanted to pack another suitcase and get on another coach. He wanted rock and chips at Baileys again. He wanted to check that I was, 'Alright for money?' He wanted to give me batteries and shoelaces and dog leads to make up for everything he never needed to make up for. Tonight I miss my dad more than ever. My dad would understand.

**March 14<sup>th</sup> Breakfast and first visit** Today Robbie and my boys, John and Chris, are coming to visit. I hand washed my black trousers during the week in case the need for them didn't coincide with one of my laundry days; mine are Tuesday and Friday. The slip confirming the visit came under my door this morning.

Today there is a competition to see who has the cleanest cell. The winner receives 75p to go into their account. I don't care about the 75p but I really want to win this competition. I started yesterday. The toothpaste on the w a l l s , used as g l u e , has been scrubbed off, s p r e a d i n g a n d leaving a powdery film. Only the cigarette burns can be seen. The bible quotes came off along with the toothpaste. I think the previous occupant must have been a religious smoker with good oral hygiene.

## OTHER USES FOR A TAMPAX

If your lighter is empty and will only issue a spark, a smoker can be driven into madness. Kirsty was driven into madness years ago and wanders around the wing, lost and isolated. Sometimes she kicks off but only mildly, repeatedly slamming her door and shouting inanely at the officers for some slight. This morning she visited Ellie's cell while I was there. Ellie is kind to Kirsty. They decided to have a smoke. Kirsty rolled a skinny prison rollie but neither had a light so she asked Ellie for a Tampax. All the cells have packets of Tampax, even mine, with an occupant who hasn't needed one since an American doctor filleted her in 1980 with the reassurance that he'd 'taken away the baby bed but left the playpen'. I laughed along with him politely, unsure of what the 'playpen' was. Kirsty took the Tampax out of its plastic cover and carefully opened it. She removed a piece of wadding and loosened it so that the air could move freely. She sparked the lighter until the wadding caught and quickly lit her cigarette. Ellie then lit hers from Kirsty's.

## THE FIRST VISIT

Robbie, John and Chris came to visit. We're searched as we walk through to the waiting area then we're called and go to the desk to have our fingerprints checked on the machine.

The hall is large with groups of armchairs and a small table in the middle of each group. The chairs all match except one that's a different colour; that's the one for the prisoner to sit on. We read the rules before we go in:

No open mouthed kissing.

No holding hands.

A cuddle and kiss to say hello and goodbye. Then the visit. Talking, enquiring, asking, and telling. All at speed. Who, what, when, how? A piece of the outside is inside. I love these three men so much. They make me proud. Robbie is so angry about it all but he knows the bottom line; Hess never goes back, no matter what. I worry that he'll cave in. An hour passes and still so much to say. I want to speak and listen at the same time. I grab everything, every detail. Ashleigh's first gig, in the mosh pit, lost her shoe. 'It was wicked Dad!'

Robbie has a gig tonight. He looked uncomfortable when I reminded him. He knows how much I love gigs and I booked this one for him.

Chris tells me that he was searched rather too closely by a female officer on the w a y  i n . She then called to her colleague, 'Do you want a piece of this?' and her colleague searched him again. My unfailingly assertive son took this in silence, not knowing how a protest would affect his mum, locked away from him behind a prison wall.

Time to go. The officer gives us a five minute warning and already I'm looking at next week's visit. They've bought me in some clothes. I'll collect them when I leave the hall. Chris s t a n d s u p t o give me a goodbye cuddle. He won't let me go. He holds on.

'It's fine,' I say. 'I'm fine. It's really not as bad as you think. The women are really friendly.' I make a joke about 6ft lesbians in showers.

'One more thing I can cross off my 50 things to do before I die list,' I say. We all smile. We wave as they leave but they linger by the door until I collect my ID badge and have my fingerprints checked again. I am sustained for a week.

I walk across the yard with the others and back to my wing. I wait at the wing door until an officer spots me and lets me in. I go back to my cell carrying my visit in a smile on my face. Some women ask me about it. 'Who came to see you?' They haven't had a visit today. I don't know when they have had a visit and I feel uncomfortable sharing my happiness with them. But they're happy for me. Why is there no envy in this place?

Robbie has bought me clothes from Marks and Spencers. Warm jogging bottoms without elasticated ankles. Hooray! T-shirts. All dark, just as I asked. I never shop in Marks and Spencers. I can't afford it.

**March 14<sup>th</sup> After lock up** Beverley is calling out, 'Goodnight Sarah, goodnight Akisha, goodnight Sacha.' It's as though we're her children and she's putting us to bed. I think Beverley would be a good mum.

**March 15<sup>th</sup>** I've just got to the bottom of this HDC or eighteen day early release. It goes like this: I can go home on April 17<sup>th</sup> with a tag on my ankle and a curfew order. The tag will come off on June 1<sup>st</sup>. The curfew is 7 pm to 7 am I believe. Or I can go home with an eighteen day early release, that's eighteen days off June 1<sup>st</sup>, which will be May 14<sup>th</sup>. This is my dilemma: if I choose the HDC of April 17<sup>th</sup> I won't be able to go to my brother's wedding reception on May 23<sup>rd</sup> because of the curfew. However if I choose the eighteen day early release I'll be in prison for an extra month but won't be tagged. Jan explained it to me as she works in reception and has been in prison many times: drink driving, borrowing money (£20) with no intention of paying it back (fraud). Jan is completely without excuses. She has a respectable life on the outside. She isn't cut or tattooed. She doesn't swear. She just can't stop drinking. When Jan is with Marion, a middle-aged, well-dressed, well-spoken woman, they do have a tendency to turn into the 'Cut Above' twins but on her own Jan is easy to reach, not hiding behind a wall of excuses and self-pity as Marion is. Jan has a son called

James who has Aspergers Syndrome and we've shared a few James/Solomon anecdotes.

Solomon, my wondrous fascinating person, told his mum that before he was born, 'When I was still in your belly,' he chose her to be his mum. 'I looked at all the others and you looked the best so I put you in a basket and kept you until I was ready to be born.' I've never heard this Buddhist teaching explained so well.

## PRISON POETRY

There are poems everywhere, on walls in corridors, in prison m a g a z i n e s, p o e t r y by w o m e n in prison. The literary snob in me came out. They rhyme. They all bloody rhyme! Words strangled, stretched, somersaulted, moved to the most impossible place, paired with the most unlikely partner: mated/related/free/splendidly/arrive/survive, bed/red. And then I saw it, the pattern, the reliability, the security of rhyme. 'Count on me,' it said. 'You can count on me.'

**March 15**<sup>th</sup> During my appeal on December 16<sup>th</sup> 2008 at Taunton Crown Court, Robbie and Tess watched as the Clerk of the Court did Christmas shopping on her laptop. Wonder who the jumper was for. Hope they kept the receipt.

**March 15<sup>th</sup> Late afternoon** It's Solomon's ninth birthday. Change the world my boy. x

### THREE PHASE DAVE

When Robbie and I were evicted, our friend Dave was told by the marina owners that Robbie and I weren't allowed to visit his boat. Dave ignored this order. He received his eviction notice in late 2008. Dave lived in a part of the marina not owned by the same people but rented by them. It was for boats that were having major work done, work that may interfere with their neighbours should it be done in the main marina.

Dave had a large wooden shed on the deck of his boat. He made it self-contained with all the home comforts. This is where he stayed when he was visiting from London, where he lived and worked as an electrician for EDF. Dave needed to have this shed lifted off and moved onto a piece of shore that was not rented by the marina owners but by someone else with whom he had arranged this move. Dave let it be known that a large crane was coming to move the shed. He'd already been refused permission to do this by the marina owners. However he was unable to get on with the conversion of his boat without the shed being moved.

The day before the crane was due to arrive, the marina owners had a large crane, which was already there, moved to a position that would block the way of the crane Dave had supposedly ordered. They also had a large piece of machinery towed around to help block the way of the crane; it was meant to be driven there but it h a d broken down on the way. However, on the day that Dave's crane was supposed to arrive, it didn't. Instead, two weeks later, a barge crane arrived and lifted Dave's shed across the water and onto t h e land. There is now has a huge piece of immovable machinery there and Dave's boat is tied up next to ours, another evictee.

**March 15<sup>th</sup> 11:00 pm** Can't sleep again. Across the yard I can see cell lights on. The night shift has put the cover across my door opening. T h i s is making me feel claustrophobic, for the first time since my ride in the tiny pod of the prison lorry. Looking out of the window helps.

Bronzefield I've been told, is the highest security category. Apparently they put the SAS in here and they had great difficulty trying to escape. I'm not sure what they were in for but it must have been something serious, two stolen dogs perhaps.

I've been pondering what to do. Should I come out on April 17<sup>th</sup> and miss John's wedding. Fran is also getting married in Cornwall on May 21<sup>st</sup> so I'd miss that one too. Or should I take the eighteen day early release which would be mid-May, make both weddings but stay in for an extra month. I'd been pondering this for days. And then I met her, the officer I wanted to punch. And I realised how quickly

I get angry. I told myself all the things I'd told Ellie, 'We can't change another person, only ourselves. Don't lose your temper. We give away our power if we do.' But I still wanted to hit her. I just can't stand rude people and I particularly loathe rude people with a bit of power. I can stomach rude people with a lot of power, except the Duke of Edinburgh.

This morning I had a 'movement' slip to see the doctor and I was trying to tell the officer. My appointment was at the beginning of the lunch break and there was a hold up. If we arrive late for an appointment we have to book another one on an 'application' form. This can take days. Iris had told me to go a bit early to miss the crush at the gates (thoughtful) but one officer decided curtly that I had to go back to class to be patted down. So I went back to be patted down. To argue would, to use a cliché, or is it a metaphor (?) fall on deaf ears. It really would be like that, with the officer not even bothering to lip read. I then returned to the gates. Officer number two decided that I had to wait until the whole section was moving. I couldn't go down a flight of stairs to 'medical'; this was not allowed, even though I'd seen individual people being let in and out of the gates during these times. This officer, for reasons I or even she may never know, decided that I had to wait. We moved, all 300 of us. Then we stopped again. There was a hold up so I asked her once more. She had closed her ears and mind to my words and they just bounced off. Her uniform seemed sharper to me then; I noticed the crease of the navy blue and the whiteness of the shirt. I may as well have been facing the razor-wired fences outside.

She knew I was angry but I remained on the safe side of rage. She wasn't going to win this war; she'd already won the battle by reminding me that there was absolutely nothing I could do. She had the uniform; I had the sentence. I realised how easy it is, once in the system, to remain in it. How easy it is to get into trouble. She was my mirror and the answer to my dilemma. I'll leave this place as soon as I can, tag or no tag, weddings or no bloody weddings.

The doctor I saw today was Dr Francis and a completely different type of human being to his colleague, who Dr Francis told me was called Dr Simon. Dr Francis spoke to me as an equal, which we are; we're both human beings. Surprisingly my blood pressure wasn't too bad, considering I'd just had murderous thoughts towards an officer. Dr Francis was efficient, reasonable and polite. I believe that's the least any of us can be towards each other. Thank you Dr Francis.

I was going to ask the probation service for special dispensation to attend my brother's wedding but as I'm not a reality star with cancer it's probably not a good idea.

**March 16<sup>th</sup> Dinner time** I've done one week in 3A. It's clean bedding and towel day. Another calendar for me to count on. How many clean towels before I go home?

## NATASHA

*Natasha is thirty-four and looks fifty. Due to her heroin addiction she, like most addicts, has lost many of her teeth, with the remaining ones either black or broken. Natasha is tiny, with the wrists of a small child. The tattooed name appears on her thin arms with the word 'princess' in dark blue calligraphy across her left forearm. Natasha is detoxed now and her feelings, her grief and losses, are trickling out, taking her by surprise. She carries with her an old, gnarled, black and white photo of her step-grandfather, someone she loved and who loved her back. When he died Natasha took heroin and began her criminality, a much less painful process than the one that forces us to remember and regret. Natasha is coming to life again and it hurts.*

**March 16<sup>th</sup> After lock up** When someone is arrested, according to the law, they have a right to make a phone call, unless of course the officer says 'no' to the request and no one cares. This is what happened to me in August 2007 when I met PC Stuart, at a prearranged time, at Bridgewater Police Station. I have told one solicitor and two barristers that I wasn't allowed to make a phone call. This is what I have learned: a prisoner in police custody has a right to make a phone call unless the call may lead to more criminality. PC Stuart explained that I couldn't make a phone call in case I asked someone to move Hess.

'Of course,' I agreed.

I have also learned that should your phone call be refused, someone has to offer to make that call for you. I also discovered that a prisoner only has the 'right' if someone decides to give it to them. If it is not given to them then they don't have it and no one cares or does anything about it.

I was questioned by PC Stuart when I went to our prearranged meeting. He asked me some questions and my answers defined the legal meaning of 'theft'. I answered each question truthfully and gave him one 'no comment' when he asked me where Hess was, then he charged me. Later in the day I was asked if I wanted a solicitor. I wasn't sure if I needed one but the officer advised me that it was probably a good idea. A solicitor was called and we had the recorded interview. I have no idea if I should have had a solicitor at the initial interview with PC Stuart and no one has questioned it.

## LOUISE

*March 17th She was working in the prison grounds, planting and weeding. She'd been described to me; pretty, long dark hair, so I called out to her and walked over. With a voice like a Welsh breeze, Louise hugged me tightly and called me 'an amazing woman'.*

'What better reason to come to prison than to stop an animal suffering,' she said.

Louise is serving eleven years for the part she played in the SHAC organization. She told me about Susan, serving two years for a dog rescue. We speak quickly, an officer watching. I'm on my way to work. We have no time to learn about each other, just rushed words and over the shoulder glances at those in charge. We'll speak again. Eleven years. How is she putting one foot in front of the other? My mind can't hold the thought. Eleven years.

## MOTHERS' DAY

Natasha showed me the Mothers' Day card that she'd made in her IT class. It's on a piece of A4 folded paper. On it is a computerised picture of flowers in a vase. Inside the card was her poem, printed onto coarse pink paper then roughly torn and glued. Prisoners aren't allowed to use scissors, except under supervision, one pair per room. I gave her a small plastic bag for the photo of her step-granddad, one of the small, sealable plastic bags that our tea, coffee and jam come in.

Yvonne showed me the large A4 sized card she'd made for her mum. On it was a picture of a convict in an arrowed suit with a ball and chain around his ankle.

There's something about making her Mothers' Day card that has given Yvonne a glow. She said that she's speaking to her mum now, since the letter.

Hearing Yvonne break down over the phone, her mum then sent her new, kinder letters, letters from a mum to a daughter. Yvonne asked me if she would need a special stamp to post the card. I said that I thought it would be OK. I gave her two 1$^{st}$ class stamps, which she twice promised to return to me on Friday, when her canteen order arrives. Yvonne is tough, hardened to prison life, in prison once again for extreme violence. Yvonne is someone that no one in here will cross. If she chooses not to return my stamps there would be nothing I could do. But she'll return them. I have no doubt. I wouldn't have missed this experience for anything. These women warm my heart and humble my soul.

I have ordered envelopes and they'll arrive on Friday. I have some stamps left. This weekend I'll write many letters: thank-yous, reassurances, guidances, letters of gratitude.

### GETTING ARRESTED

**March 17$^{th}$ After lock up** Getting arrested wasn't easy for me. On Sunday August 19$^{th}$ 2007, I placed Hess with Maria and drove myself to the shiny new Bridgewater Police Station.

'I understand you're looking for me,' I told the rather rotund officer behind the counter, 'about a dog.'

'A dog?'

'Yes. I've rescued a dog and apparently the police have been looking for me.'

I did speak with a police officer while I was on the run. He did his best to persuade me to come back, at one point suggesting, 'Perhaps you could share the dog.'

But when I said that I had been looking after Hess for two months he hesitated for a second and then continued with his script. Clearly no one had told him.

I felt a bit sorry for him and thought, 'Bless you. You really don't want to be doing this do you?'

'I'll just check the computer,' PC Rotund said.

'No, you're not on the computer.'

I wasn't sure if this meant that I didn't exist or that I wasn't on Britain's Most Wanted list after all. I wanted it on the record that I had gone to the police station so I insisted that he flag it on the computer. Then I went home and the next day I received a message on my phone to call another officer. When I called the number an answer machine came on. I wasn't having much luck getting arrested. And on Tuesday August 21st 2007 the legal machine kicked into life. A phone call from PC Stuart. He was on his way to Clevedon.

'Do you have the dog?' he asked.

'No.'

'Where is it?'

'I'm sorry. I can't tell you.'

'Is it in Clevedon?'

'No, he's not in Clevedon.'

'Are you sure because I'm halfway there and if I find out it's there and you're lying, you're going to be in trouble.'

'I can assure you, he's not in Clevedon.'

Now Hess is 'property' as far as the police and CPS are concerned but his value, according to the court on July 1st 2008, is £0. So what was it about this dog that would make the local police drive fifty miles to find him? And why wouldn't they simply call the local Clevedon police and ask them to check an address for a stolen mongrel? Now that's a conversation I'd love to hear.

PC Stuart and I meet at 11 am. He is a friendly young man and we chat about the black Labrador he hopes to buy when he moves in with his girlfriend. I suggest to him that he rescues one. 'Perhaps not the way I did,' I say. We both smile. Then the short interview during which time he tries to persuade me to return Hess. The desk sergeant also tries, threatening me with prison. 'Scare tactics!' I think. I'm then put in a cell at 12:00 am after I've been charged, fingerprinted, DNA'd and photographed. I have to leave my shoes outside. Copious cups of tea are brought in and I'm treated courteously. A civilian employee comes into my cell, sits on the bunk and says, 'What's all this about then?' I tell him about Hess and Veronica. He says, 'That's exactly what my wife would do.' We then realise that we used to be neighbours. That night he went home and told his wife that I'd been charged with dog theft.

'Lin hasn't stolen a dog; she's rescued one,' his wife said, without needing to listen to the story.

At some point during the day PC Stuart told me that he had to call the CPS to see if they wanted to go ahead with the case. He returned shortly afterwards to tell me that they did. I had a long, taped interview and at 9 pm I was taken to the front desk and told that I had to appear in Bridgewater Magistrates' Court the following Monday. I believe this was in order for me to answer the charge. After signing many p i e c e s of paper I thought I was going to be released. But PC Stuart realised that no bail conditions had been set.

'What about bail conditions Sarge?' he said, bright-eyed, to the old grizzled sergeant. It was reminiscent of Hill Street Blues. The sergeant stared at him over his glasses.

'I know. How about, she can't take the dog abroad?' PC Stuart suggested, as though Hess and I were about to flee to Marbella and sun it up with the rest of the criminal fraternity.

'But I wouldn't do that,' I said. 'I'd never be able to get him in the photo booth.'

I watched PC Stuart cement his mouth into a fixed line and the bail conditions were set. No Pina Coladas for Hess and me just yet.

When I arrived home to the boat that night Robbie was having guitar practice with Alan, the lead guitarist in his band. They had a Cornwall tour coming up and guitar practice just couldn't be cancelled; those numbers had to be right. Robbie made a cup of tea for us all.

**March 18<sup>th</sup> Lunchtime I've** b e e n  m o v e d again, this time to block 2C. There appears to be no logic to the moves as Ellie is being moved too and she's going home in two days. I believe they move me because I clean each cell when I arrive. If they keep moving me, eventually they'll have a sparkling clean prison. The marigold gloves on the bunk should have been a clue. Two very friendly women in here so far. Lots of toothpaste on the walls, in fact there must be tubes of it but this time I refuse to clean it off. It's very quiet in here. Most people are at work.

**March 18<sup>th</sup> Dinner time** Loud, raucous, experienced, cocky, that's the population of 2C. Large women queuing up for seconds while the new ones wait in line for firsts. And the worst thing of all, officers too weak or disinterested to care. For the first time since I arrived, I fear that I won't be able to do my time.

I haven't missed a Gongyo since I've been here, despite often having to be in three places at the same time and now it feels as though the universe is saying, 'OK. You've managed so far. Let's see what you're really made of. Now try this lot!' I struggle to remember that this is the Buddha land because I'm here chanting. And so is Ellie now.

## IN THE SHOWER

A young, skinny, toothless woman tried to make me feel welcome. I must have looked scared.

'It's alright in here,' she said, smiling. I felt grateful to her and remembered Janet Marshall's guidance, 'It's just about that one person standing in front of us in that moment.' To make a heart to heart connection in some way, large or small, to share something with another person, this is the basis of everything that is important. This particular person was sopping wet with a towel around her and concern in her face. And this person, for no reason, tried to remove my fear and replace it with reassurance.

When I went back to my cell Alice saw me washing the cover of my fan and came in for a chat. I have two friends in here now, Ellie and Alice. Perhaps we're moved so that we don't make friends. Friendship is powerful and we're not supposed to have any power in here.

The showers in here are better than the one on the boat. At least the temperature doesn't change when someone fills a kettle. I'll be OK. I'll be fine. The knowledge that I can go free if I say where Hess is makes me the only prisoner here by choice and this makes me feel stronger. Perhaps that's why Judge Simpton was so angry with me. The only thing he had to punish me with was imprisonment and I chose to take it.

## STRESS MANAGEMENT

During Iris' stress management class this afternoon the Prison Governor came through the Education block and popped her head around the door.

'What class is this?' she asked.

'Stress management,' Iris replied.

'Any tips on how to relieve stress?' she continued, impressing the important visitor she had with her.

'Yes. Stop moving us around every few days or at least tell us why you're doing it,' I said.

**March 18<sup>th</sup> 10:45 pm** From my new window I can see how close I am to the outside. Fifteen yards away is the first wire fence, thirty feet high, of closely woven mesh. Too tight for a finger hold. Beyond that is the second fence, also thirty feet high, with rolls of razor wire on top, then the third barrier, a solid steel fence, to hide us from the innocent. I just wonder, if my life depended on it, could I scale these barriers?

**March 18<sup>th</sup> Late I think** Each week we're given a menu so that we can choose and plan our following week's meals. (Mr Littlejohn has just clasped his chest! It's OK; he's being given first aid by Kelvin Mackenzie. Melanie Phillips has gone to call an ambulance.) Our new menu begins on Mondays, so this Monday my week of 'Healthy Options' began. This is the first week that I've actually been able to choose my food because each time we're moved around we have to take up the menu of the prisoner whose cell we've taken over. So I hope the woman who took over Cell 17, Block 3A is enjoying my tuna wraps and egg salads. Unfortunately the person whose cell I now occupy wasn't too concerned about healthy food; my dinner tonight was sausages and chips so I now have another week of confused and reluctant bowels.

## NATASHA

*March 19<sup>th</sup>* *Natasha had a visit yesterday and returned to the class carrying a mouthful of bitterness. Her brother, 'The only man I trust,' she said, told her that her ex-husband, who'd moved into her flat while she was in prison, has thrown all of her belongings in the bin.*

*'Clothes, CDs, everything.'*

*'Why was he living in your flat?' I asked.*

*'He promised he'd look after it and my son while I was in here. Now the cunt's thrown my stuff out and told my son that I've abandoned him.'*

*Natasha's brother also told her that a petition had gone around the estate demanding that the Housing Association evict her and her family. An eviction notice has been served on her family.*

*'They've washed their hands of us.'*

*'Can your brother speak to your son and explain to him that you haven't abandoned him?'*

'He already has but it's confusing him. I haven't abandoned him. I'm in prison. That bastard's stabbed me in the back!'

When I'm raging, as Natasha was, the last thing I want to hear in the midst of it is something 'positive'. I'd positively tell them to piss off. So I thought, churned and chanted in my head, then I stepped back. On the way back to the block I spoke to Natasha.

'At least you know now Natasha. You can't rely on your ex when you're in trouble. You don't have to bother with him anymore. You don't have to waste any more time or energy on him.'

Not original, trite really, but a true thought. Natasha is a sparky, bright, fearsomely strong woman. Even in here she seems to hang onto herself. Her fire shows in her eyes but not as a defence, like so many in here, but because she naturally burns with a determination to get it right this time, for herself and for her children.

**March 19<sup>th</sup> Lunchtime** My canteen has arrived. It consists of: £10 in phone credits, which I'm building up by saving a few from the previous week, for the urgent times when I just need to speak with Robbie. There are also thirty envelopes for my weekend of letter writing and a lime green Wisdom toothbrush. The grey prison issue toothbrush c a n now be binned. Using it isn't unlike brushing with a long dead hedgehog. (A new writing pad started. Where will I be when I come to the end of this one?)

105

The daffodils are out in the gardens and I pass them going to and from work. I want to touch one, just to feel it, but I don't know if it's against the rules. Ellie is released tomorrow. I'm going to ask her to buy some daffodils for herself. She deserves some daffodils.

This afternoon I went to the 'Life Stories' workshop, which is run by a writer in residence called Beth. In the group was a black American woman called Rose. Rose was hungry she said, and 'close to the edge'. She'd found a hair in her food at lunchtime and had been unable to eat. Beth found her someone to talk to and she left the room, returning later, towards the end of the hour.

We did some writing exercises, the first linked to an 'icebreaker', during which we walked around the room asking each other set questions: Do you live alone? Do you collect things? The second piece of writing was linked to a postcard we'd selected from the fifty or so Beth had spread across the floor. The woman called Amanda asked me if I was, 'Lin, the dog rescue woman?'

'I'm Amanda. One of Louise's co- defendants,' she said and shook my hand firmly. I felt faintly warmed that she knew of me but we don't appear to have anything in common. Amanda is a vegan of course and much braver than me. She's doing many years in here, for a principle. But probably the most striking difference is that Amanda wears lycra shorts and works in the gym, whereas I view a gym as I would an abattoir; I know they exist but I wouldn't want to go in one.

**Sally** Is Indian with a Glaswegian accent. I hoped she was also a Celtic supporter but didn't appear interested when I mentioned the 'b h o y s'. She wrote a beautiful piece about her parents' love affair, 'started in primary school and the talk of the village'. I assumed that I would be the best writer in the group. I really need to be in Bronzefield. My ego needs to be picked up and shaken; the rest of me has so why not this bit too?

**Sheila** Wears her abuse like a robe and speaks as though it is the most interesting thing about her, as though it defines her. She loves an audience and speaks in that practised matter of fact way used for effect. She mildly irritated me and I deliberately listened to her s t o r i e s with the same deadpan expression that she used. If Beth isn't careful these sessions could easily become the place where people compete to see who suffered the worst abuse.

When I returned to the block Ellie came up to me carefully holding a still wet painting, thick in black and gold paint. On it was a cut-out dragonfly.

'I made it for you,' she said. 'Careful, it's still wet.'

One of the officers gave me a key to my cell today. Then he said, 'I've put your Independent on the bed and your key is by the telly.' It felt a bit like home but with better manners.

**March 19<sup>th</sup> Lock up** Some of the women in 2C have found out why I'm here and I'm getting some cuddles, strange, nice, but sort of OK. I appear to be a bit of an anomaly in Bronzefield. I am the only prisoner who is here by choice so I'm treated like something odd that's been found in a field, with curiosity and a bit of hesitation. Robbie has said that's how many people treat me because I scare them. What they don't know, in prison and out, is how much I want them to come up to me, cross the barrier of my fear, and join me on the other side.

**March 20<sup>th</sup>** Today it was decided that I had to be a 'proper' teacher and not simply 'assist'. I was cheaper than employing a supply teacher for the day I assume. Joe was on a course so Iris took his class and I took Iris'. I was in the classroom, unsupervised, with women asking for permission to go to the toilet.

'I'm a prisoner just like you. You don't have to ask me if you can go to the toilet,' I told them.

I was trusted not to plot our escape. Instead we all went on our holidays, some remembered, some imagined. We skied down mountains and swam in turquoise seas. We covered ourselves with lotion smelling of wild flowers; it eased our sunburn. For a while we all climbed over those walls. And no one could catch us.

**March 21st After breakfast** Food appears to be an issue in 2C. On my first day in here, while in the dinner line, someone said, 'There's never enough food in here.' I disagree. We can all survive on what we're given but the tastes and trading, make food distribution uneven.

## CHRISTINE

*Christine is a brash young black woman with a strong survival instinct. She arrived at the same time as me and we did our induction together. Christine is mouthy but not crude. She's confident and pushy. Khadra is also in 2C and Christine has been asking for the things that Khadra doesn't eat; biscuits and crisps.*

*I was in the dinner queue with both of them last night. Fresh fruit is scarce in Bronzefield but yesterday I'd stored an orange for a later time. When Christine began asking Khadra for her food, Khadra pretended that she didn't understand, then she gave her items to me, possibly because I've been helping her fill out her applications and write her letters, possibly not. When I told Christine that I didn't eat bread she jumped on it.*

*'I'll have your roll then.'*

*'OK. Take it off my plate when I get it.'*

*'No. I need to have it put in my hand. I don't take anything off people's plates,' she said, looking at my plate as though it was a drain cover.*

*Christine came up to the servery counter with me and when they handed me the roll, Christine quickly took it but the officer noticed.*

109

*'Are you bullying her?' he said.*

*'No!' Christine told him. 'She said I could have it. Tell her I'm not bullying you,' she ordered. Bullying is jumped on in Bronzefield. I went back to the server.*

*'I don't eat bread. I told her she could have it.'*

Then something curious happened. I realised that I could no longer be bullied. I felt completely unafraid and realised that I wouldn't let anyone bully me, in Bronzefield or anywhere.

Khadra is eating very little and I'm worried for her and her baby. I called to her across the balcony as she was going into her cell. I held out my orange.

*'No,' she said. 'It's OK.'*

*'For your baby,' I said and gave her the orange.*

The oddest thing about Christine is that when I asked her name she didn't ask mine. This hasn't happened before but I don't think Christine needs to know my name, or anyone else's. She just needs to survive and her delicate footprints can be seen on the backs of many in here.

Last night I received a card from Nepal. Hima is there and had many SGI members sign it. There is a Nepalese woman in 2C. She gets drunk at home and is violent towards her husband and children. I showed her the card and she kissed the stamps on the envelope. I also received another book and card from Leah and Ben. On the card is a stylised drawing of a dog by a river, looking across at a boat. The picture is called 'Waiting'. I know that they selected

110

this card very carefully for me; they were thinking of Bob waiting by my boat for my return. I wish I could be that thoughtful towards people.

Yesterday I wrote twenty-five letters. I want to send at least one letter to each person who is writing to me. I haven't counted my cards and letters but they are running into the hundreds and each time I'm moved, the bag I carry them in gets heavier.

This morning Ha, a Vietnamese woman who has been in my ESOL class, knocked on my door and asked me if I would teach her English. I was annoyed and now understand Lizzie and the extra stamp. To offer is entirely different to being asked. When asked, it feels as though the little I have of me is being taken. Time is more precious to me than food. If I offer it to someone it's because I can spare it or want to share it.

**March 21<sup>st</sup>** My visit has been booked for 12:30. Lunch is at 12:00. Today 'upstairs' is first in the queue. If I was 'downstairs' would I have to choose between a visit and food? No one has told me what to do. I don't mind going hungry. I'll swap food for a cuddle.

**The visit** Justine and Caz came but Katy, they told me, was stuck in traffic on the M5 and they weren't sure if she'd be allowed in. Katy arrived with George and Isla halfway through the visit. I know Isla has been worried about me.

111

We caught up as best we could. Justine and Caz seemed quite fascinated with the details of prison life. When they left I collected the package that Katy had brought for me; in it were envelopes, paper and stamps...except there were no stamps. I don't know where my stamps are and I have no way of finding out. I feel cut off, angry. My Visitors Order has gone out in a 'free' letter now as I have no stamp. I hope it arrives. Next week it's Robbie, John and Karen.

Just spoke with Katy on the phone. This week the stamp routine had been changed. She was told to put them in an envelope and post them internally. I should get them in a few days. Last week they were in the package with everything else.

**March 21<sup>st</sup> Dinner time** The woman prisoner who is dishing up in servery remembered that I don't eat bread. She's quite concerned and is trying to organize a special pack for me. Bless her.

**March 22<sup>nd</sup> Breakfast** A dark, dwarf-like woman, part male, part female, knocked on my door as soon as it was unlocked.

'Excuse me. Do you have a Rizla please?'

'I don't smoke. Sorry.'

The same vague mistrust mixed with surprise swept across her face and was gone, along with her. As she's a 'chancer' she won't speak to me again. A non-smoker is an extremely small minority among the British women in prison. Each time I come into my cell the smell is here. No matter how long I'm in here, it will never go. It's in the walls, the grubby beige curtains, the mattress. Last night I was down scrubbing the floor again and for a few moments the smell is gone.

Over my bed is a large toothpaste heart, formed by a previous occupant. Inside it I have stuck a photo of Bob. Is it a human need to want to create a home wherever we are? I wonder if the men's prisons are covered in pictures of children, flowers painted in art class and hearts drawn in toothpaste.

## LITTLE JOHN

He was nearly five months old when we moved into that house and two years and six months when I left him there, with his dad, for the first time. I kept going back to be near him but I knew I couldn't stay.

His dad, Big John, had gone out to buy wallpaper for Little John's room and returned a few hours later with paper covered in shooting rockets and planets. Perfect for an eight year old but for a five month old I was hoping for something gentler. But the paper stayed up and saw Little John through his shooting rockets years. His was the first room we decorated in that large Victorian terrace we'd managed to buy for £4,600, with a mortgage from the Guardian Building Society and a loan for the deposit from Mr Gold, Big John's boss.

When Little John was two weeks old I began working at home, overlocking garments for Stylerite, Mr Gold's company, which was just off Mare Street in Hackney. We were living in two rooms and a kitchen, four flights up over a cafe in Stoke Newington, owned by a family of Greek Cypriots. It cost £5 a week and we were lucky to get it. There was no bath or shower and the toilet, shared by the other tenants, was three flights down and inhabited by a thick limbed spider. Consequently my toilet habits were fast and completed with my legs bent and feet off the floor.

In our flat lived a nation of red ants which showed themselves for the first time when I retrieved a birthday cake I'd bought for Big John from the top of the cupboard. The white icing had turned into a rusty orange, undulating ocean.

I hated the house as soon as we'd bought it and moved in. It wasn't the ice-cold rooms that we just couldn't afford to heat; I simply felt an animosity towards me and a tragedy that the walls were trying to tell. Outside our bedroom door, on the landing, was the worst place. There, an unspeakable suffering lingered and I always expected to find someone hanging. Many years after I'd moved out, Mary, Big John's sister-in-law, stayed in that house. On their return from the off-licence, Big John and his brother Jim, Mary's husband, found her standing on the doorstep, refusing to stay in the house alone. I had never spoken to Mary about how I felt.

I was seventeen and a month when I met Big John. We became engaged on my eighteenth birthday. A party, held in the Lord Stanley, moved on to the basement flat Big John shared with three other lads from Glasgow. For years afterwards we would talk about that party.

'Even Auntie Vera grabbed a crate of beer and carried it down the road.'

We married on March 25$^{th}$ 1967 and Little John was born on July 3$^{rd}$ 1968. I was nineteen and Big John almost twenty-four. Many people assumed that I was pregnant when we married and I enjoyed saying, 'The longest pregnancy in history. Only an elephant has a longer one.'

The birth was long and difficult with two doctors finally having to pull him out with forceps, ripping me inside and out.

The maternity wing of Hackney Hospital was the place they sent women to ensure they would never want to have another child. During my twenty-four hour labour I was left alone, no parents or husbands were allowed. Two nurses were sent in to me at one point and fell asleep, one with her head on my bed. A sister came in.

'Can I have something for the pain please?'

'No. We gave you something and it slowed down your labour.'

'But it hurts.'

'Well it does hurt having a baby dear, didn't anyone tell you that?'

She had an ice-cold look, an efficient and resentful woman, resentful of the inconvenience caused by women having babies. I didn't ask again. She came in later to tell me that my baby was 'in distress' but I didn't know what she meant. When I heard a woman sobbing across the hall I asked a nurse what was wrong with her.

'Her baby died. It's her own fault. She didn't come to any antenatal check-ups. '

I'd always told Big John that I didn't want children, 'but I'd have a puppy if I could. ' And I knew, as soon as Little John was born, that my love for him was far stronger than my capacity to be a good mum, that these two things are not mutually inclusive. Big John came from a large, non-practising Catholic family. Not wanting children was like not wanting water, unnatural.

The regime in the maternity wing was stringent. If a mother missed the nappy trolley, the baby remained in the soiled one or stayed un-nappied until the trolley did its rounds again. I was given an injection to knock me out after the birth and when I woke up I was in a ward with another woman and her twin baby girls. A nurse sat me on the bedpan on a chair but I kept falling off because I was still drowsy from the injection. I was on fire and the pain was like nothing I'd felt before.

'If you don't pass water I'll have to catheterize you,' the nurse warned, as though my retention of water was a personal slight. I just couldn't do it, and

116

the next morning she slipped a rubber hose into the hole created and held together with tight stitches, as the tears crept down my face. I didn't make a sound. It wasn't determination or stubbornness but fear of the wrath of the nurse, my jailer, in a place from which I could not escape.

The worst treatment was for the unmarried mothers or those unable or unwilling to breastfeed. I appeared to be doing everything right. I was a married, breastfeeding mother who never made a fuss. But still I was punished, as was my baby, for being there and inconveniencing an otherwise spotless and seamless routine.

I didn't know this wasn't supposed to happen until five years later when I gave birth to Christopher in Whipps Cross Hospital, encouraged by gentle and smiling nurses who shared in my joy.

In 1972 Hackney Hospital was performing operations on women to unblock their fallopian tubes. These were being performed without an anaesthetic. I was scheduled to have this procedure and when I asked the doctor if it would hurt he said, 'Yes'. No reassurance that they would do everything they could to ease the pain. But fortunately I needed another procedure at the same time so I was anaesthetised. I wonder how many women went through the agony of this, completely unaware that it didn't have to be so.

Two weeks after I'd given birth, Big John collected us from the hospital in his white, works Transit van. I didn't realise that there was a name for the fear and shame that left hospital with us. It's only with the distance of years that I can see the monster lurking under the surface. There wasn't a name for it then and even if there had been I couldn't have seen it through my guilt.

**March 22<sup>nd</sup> Afternoon** It's the noise. If anyone asks me, it's the noise, that's the worst thing about prison. Despite being only 50% of this prison population, 100% of the noise comes from the young, white, English women. They walk around the prison with their necks out and their fists clenched. I imagine that is how they walk through life. They don't speak, they shout, all the time. They can't stop shouting or moving around. They're unable to concentrate for longer than a few seconds. They ask a question then cut off the answer, unable to listen. I expect, if I Google it, I'll find a syndrome that fits them.

This is the last complete week of March 2009. When April arrives I'll begin to think about home and being there.

Today is Mothers' Day and each of us had two daffodils in bud left on the floor outside our cell. It felt almost mocking, this thoughtful gesture, like falling in love just before being told we have a terminal illness.

But at least while I'm in prison I have no internet access, which means that I don't have to read those dreadful 'inspirational' emails that make me want to pull out my eyes and eat them. I receive them

118

regularly from people who believe they know me, without realising that the sending of the email demonstrates they clearly don't. Robbie told me that someone has even sent me one when they know I'm in prison. It said, 'If you forward this to ten other people something wonderful will happen to you today.' He replied by saying, 'Please print out this email, piss on it and eat it.' I usually just delete them.

There's another pattern emerging in here. The young women never take Home Detention Curfew. They take the extra time and go out without a tag. Many of them are here for drug offences and shoplifting. To be released and have to stay in at night, that time when for many of them, the day begins, would be like torture. It would simply be another prison sentence, watching their friends in the pubs and clubs, the park, roaming around looking for the colour and sound of life, while all they can do is look at the night from a window. The window may as well have bars.


**March 22$^{nd}$ 10:00 pm Vital** that's one word I would use to describe prison – vital. In the morning I go down to breakfast and there's a new face in the queue. I come back from work and someone has gone, never to meet again. No time to learn more about them or give out a phone number. I gave my number to Alice as soon as she gave her fruit to Khadra. That act told me that I liked her, could trust her. In a place where fruit is at a premium, one word from me and she gave her fruit to a woman she didn't even know.

'She needs it more than I do,' she said, without a hint of self-aggrandisement.

We can afford to give when we know more is available, a walk to the shops. But Alice just gave hers and once more I feel so grateful to have met these people. What I see is that the people in here are no different to those on the outside; some will give their last and some will grab what they can. I know those at both ends but I believe most of us fall somewhere in the middle.


**March 23<sup>rd</sup> between lunch and lock up** Alice came into my cell to give me an orange. I wanted to chat with her so she sat on my bunk. Drugs are the reason she's in prison. Alice doesn't know her dad. He left when her mother was three months pregnant with her. She has a sister who she doesn't know. Her sister's father (Alice has a different father to her sister) was shot dead by his brother, who also killed his own wife, with whom his brother was sleeping. Then he killed himself. Alice has been told that her father, 'was away with the fairies' and that he believed aliens were following him. Alice's mother has manic depression and Alice feels that she may also have it.

'One minute I'm so happy I could scream. The next minute I'm crying and I don't know why.'

She told me all of this as though we'd known each other for a long time. No drama, no self-pity. I really like this woman.

Before she left, Ellie found an extra flask and gave it to me. Now I have two. Last night I cut my finger on one and discovered that there was a jagged split along the bottom. It's lethal, at least in here it is. For the self-harmer it could provide hours of amusement. For those women whose violence goes outwards and not in, a vein could be opened or a face rutted before an officer could stop it. I've decided to keep it. I have no trust in the competence of the officers in 2C to dispose of it safely.

## SUDDENLY

**March 24<sup>th</sup>** Suddenly is an adverb. When teaching, Iris often uses our own situation, prison, as an example. Yesterday she put 'suddenly' into context for us.

'When you came to prison, it was suddenly? One minute in court, then prison? Suddenly? Quickly, yes?' she went on.
It's strange how we seem to lapse into broken English when speaking with a foreigner. Even Iris, the English teacher, did this. Prepositions don't seem necessary. Verbs are guillotined.

'You go prison *suddenly*?' She continued. 'Khadra, how did you get here?'

'They tell me. . . . . '

'They *told* you Khadra. It's the past tense.'

121

'They *told* me I going for. . . '

'*Was* . . . they told me *I was*. . . '

'They told me I *was* going for interview.'

Iris let Khadra's omission of t h e  indefinite article 'an' pass.

'Then I saw two police and. . . '

Khadra put her wrists together to show that she'd been handcuffed.

'They tell me interview but take me prison.'

'Yes,' said Iris, 'so that was *suddenly*.'

'Yes, *suddenly*,' Khadra quietly replied, '*suddenly*.'


**March 24th After dinner** Some prisons have a system called *Email A Prisoner*, whereby we can receive emails if the sender has signed up. The email is printed out and given to us with the rest of our post. Of course, we're unable to send emails, despite what the right wing press try to claim; that old 'holiday camp' cliché. I'd hate to stay in any of those holiday camps. At least in Bronzefield we aren't forced to get up at 6 am to play water polo with a balloon.

Tonight Chris' email arrived and I need to be with him. Tony Dawson, his best friend from Poole Grammar School, was found dead on Saturday night. It's been nearly twenty years since I last saw him but as soon as I read the email Tony's face came to me, as clearly as if he was standing in front of me. Many of the Poole Grammar School boys smoked weed; Chris was in this group. I don't know what else they did. I didn't know they did any of it but I remember the day I

122

discovered what he'd been doing and threw him out. He was about sixteen and he went to stay with his girlfriend and her parents in their large tasteful house in Poole. Chris came back home after a few days and promised not to do drugs again.

I remember Tony as being my favourite of Chris' friends. There was innocence about him, at least, that's how he looked, innocent and naive and perhaps I was right. All the other lads are walking around carrying their lives. Tony is dead, drugs probably. The other lads had a line they drew or someone drew for them. Tony seemed to drift off. His wit and intellect, his solid friendships, his life, none of this was enough for him.

### HUNTED

**March 25**[th] It's been tracking me down for a couple of days and I was managing to outrun it. Last night it caught up with me. I really have no words for it and prison is as good a place as any to spend my time with it. I don't want to speak with a 'listener' or the Samaritans. I don't want to be placated, understood, sympathised with, empathised with or any other 'ised' with. I just want to cuddle my dog under the quilt and wait for it to pass. Robbie always calls it my 'hunted' look and that's how I feel, hunted. Trying to explain it, trying to look for a reason for it is impossible. It's about all the cruelty in the world and wanting it to stop. It's sheep ripped from fields and squeezed into trucks. It's dogs tied up in sheds,

123

waiting. It's children in black wellies, standing alone in a playground. It's Christmas Carols in primary school and one shepherd in the Nativity, who no one has come to watch. If all the cruelty and sadness in the world stopped, then this would stop. If everyone and everything was warm and fed and loved, there would be no sadness. This shouldn't be called bipolar disorder; it should be called 'needing everything to be loved disorder'.

My faith teaches that each tiny action changes everything and so I do small things in the hope of adding to the huge change that must be happening. Very early in my relationship with Robbie he found me feeding a stray cat in the marina. He was irritated and said, 'Are you going to feed every stray animal you find?'

'Yes,' I said. I don't think he understood.

**March 25<sup>th</sup>** Tomorrow morning I won't be going to work, which means I'll be locked in my cell as a punishment. The reason I won't be going to work is because I have no clothes. The reason I have no clothes is because my clothes washing days are Tuesdays and Fridays and I did as I was told. First thing on Tuesday morning I took my washing to the wing laundry room. Each wing has a laundry room and a prisoner has the job of doing the laundry, except our knickers, which they won't wash. In 1A our laundry was completed and we could collect it on the same day that we put it in. So far I have twice asked the laundry woman for my

124

laundry and I've twice asked an officer; still no laundry. So in the morning, when they notice that my name has not been ticked off for work, I'll be paid a visit and that's when I'll get their attention and possibly my laundry.

**March 26<sup>th</sup> Lunchtime** Chickened out of refusing to work, rinsed out some clothes and dried them by the fan. I am so gutless. Today I got back my laundry and from now on I'll wash everything in the sink of my cell and hang it up to dry where I can. Think I'm missing a T-shirt. The young woman in charge of laundry is completely overwhelmed. I told her I'd help her to catch up at the weekend. Bugger! Wish I hadn't said that.

Iris was angry today. Combined with her usual rudeness and spitefulness there was an added sense of her own power to do with us just as she wished. I had a talk with myself and, as I'm much saner today, I made some sense. The students really don't like her but are in no position to do anything. They rebel as they can; a raised eyebrow, a word in a foreign language, a look, a smile.

## PRISON IS A NOUN

Prison is a noun that is used frequently in Iris' lessons. Question and answer sessions are built around this noun.

**Iris:**     What did you do this weekend Sonya? What did you do?

**Sonya:** I see my husband for a visit.

**Iris:** No, I *saw* my husband for a visit; it's the past tense.

We were having a lesson in *place* and *tense*.

**Iris:** I went home at the weekend but you stayed in prison. Say it! Did you go home at the weekend Adriana?

**Adriana:** No, I stay in prison.

**Iris:** 'You *stayed* in prison; it's the past tense.'

Galina was called out of class to see someone. When she returned she was very aware that she was (is?) in prison, as she sobbed her way through her place in the present tense.

'I am crying for my children,' she said.

### THE BUBBLE THEORY

**March 26th** When Iris was teaching our 'stress management' course last week she explained how she could listen to someone's problems but not absorb them and in that way they can't have a 'negative' effect on her life. In this way her 'energy' remains positive.

'It's like putting me in a bubble,' she explained. 'I can listen but I don't let it get to me; it sort of bounces off.'

Iris has been trained well and I'm certain that this method can be found in one of her many self-help books that fill her stripped pine bookshelves. Iris' life is a success.

**March 27<sup>th</sup>** Today it was decided that I should teach Joe's class, whose students aren't as advanced in English as they are in Iris' class. I was given a 'lesson plan' and a classroom assistant called Catherine, a stunningly beautiful young Irish woman who was brought up for most of her life in Columbia. Catherine is lovely and kind and quietly spoken. Her sentence is four years, her boyfriend's eight years because 'he planned it all'. I suspect Catherine is in for drug smuggling but while here she's hoping to complete a teaching qualification.

In the class today were three Chinese women, two Vietnamese, two African, two Spanish and one Italian. The Italian woman had a 'movement' slip but when she arrived at her appointment there was no one to translate, so she was sent back to class.

One of the Chinese women has been told, for the past week, that she's going to be released. Her 'movement' slip to see probation was for 9:45. On her return to the classroom she sat down and tried to catch up with her work but she was crying. Probation has told her that she isn't being released after all as immigration has changed their mind. Is immigration a 'their' or an 'it'? It appears to have no logic or heart so 'it' may be the correct pronoun after all.

What I've noticed is how quietly the women in here cry, almost secretly, as though it breaches a prison rule. I can't speak her language and she can't speak mine. All I can do is give her a tissue and touch her hand. That's the language we share.

**March 27<sup>th</sup> After lunch lock up** One of the hard women in 2C was in the second phone booth on the wing. I was in the first, speaking with my sister. I turned around and found myself facing her, with just the clear glass of two phone booths between us. She was crying. A word, a connection with home, a child, a mum, a lover, and the walls and wire and locks are circled in black felt tip. And the tears come.

**March 27<sup>th</sup> 5:00 pm After lock up** I have received an email from Robbie. The email response to his request for tomorrow's visit hadn't arrived by 12:30 today. He phoned but got the usual answer phone. I now have no idea if my visit tomorrow will go ahead and I'm locked in my cell with no way of finding out. It's going to be a long fourteen and a half hours until I can phone him.

Sometimes, in the middle of the night, a lone scream rings out and a door is pounded, over and over again. I want to scream and pound my door. It's not the visit, it's the not knowing, the space between our question and their answer; a space where we sit and rock. Is there anywhere left on earth that works on words and eye contact and touches and skin? Is there anywhere left? I will chant with determination for my

128

visit to happen. Is this a compromise? I hope not. Compromise is not my strong point.

Sometimes (often) I will have imaginary conversations in my head. Does anyone else do that? Oh, just me then. Sometimes I'm in front of a judge, and I expect I'll find myself in front of some on my release, people who judge. The conversations may go like this:

'So what would you do differently next time?'

Of course there will always be a next time, not the same circumstances but there will always be another suffering animal.

'I'd call the RSPCA and then wait for the dog to die.'

God, I'm so angry with that organisation! If they did their job we'd have more empty cells for the really serious crime of not paying the TV licence.

Khadra now has company. She has been moved to a double cell which she shares with another Somalian woman called Atash, who is serving fourteen months for child trafficking. Atash smuggled her friend's baby nephew into the UK from Somalia. His father had been killed and his mother was having difficulty keeping her four children fed. The baby was the youngest and the most vulnerable. He is now with his aunt in London.

## Plight

Many people, when writing to me, have taken to using the word 'plight' when referring to my

129

imprisonment. They appear to see something in this that I don't and are very angry on my behalf. Although I don't feel that it is a 'plight', the word could be useful when writing a prison poem, as there are so many words that rhyme with it:

*'Right'* – I always am.
*'Flight'* – to be used with *'took'* to describe my action when I did a runner with Hess.
*'Bight'* – if I wish to include something about the shipping forecast.


**March 28<sup>th</sup> Before breakfast** I've just woken up and on the floor by the door, (I'm really getting good at this rhyming!) is confirmation of my visit today, plus a VO for next week.


**Methadone** Each morning at about 10 am an officer walks around the Education Block. He stops at each room, puts his head around the door and says, 'Anyone for methadone?' One morning I'm going to take him up on his offer.


**March 29<sup>th</sup> After lunch** I thought Robbie looked thin and exhausted yesterday when I saw him and my mind decided that it was my fault. I cried for most of last night, minus one hour because the clocks sprung forward. I wrote some letters, slept after breakfast and then phoned Robbie. He tells me that actually he's put on weight and is now 15 stone. Fat bastard! Everyone is inviting him over for dinner because they're worried about him and how he's coping. Yes, he's tired because he's been working long hours and writing some songs. Bugger! All that guilt just wasted. I could have used it on something else, such as not being sexually abused as a child.

Cell 16 is now occupied by Paula, a thirty-three year old mother of four, who managed to tell me her complete life story in thirty three seconds.

'It's good to have someone sensible to talk to, not like these silly girls in here,' she told me.
Oh no, she sees me as 'sensible'. I hope that doesn't translate to 'counsellor'.


## PAULA

*Paula has been given three years instead of four and a half because she pleaded guilty. She is on the methadone program after an eight year heroin addiction. She grabbed a woman's bag and 'accidentally' dragged her into a moving van. She was caught on CCTV. The handbag was never found. Inside it was a photo of the woman's late husband, the only photo of him that she owned. Paula's victim is now too afraid to leave the house. Paula has decided that while she is doing her time, her first prison sentence, she will get clean and sign up for as many courses as she can. The sister of Paula's sixty year old boyfriend is caring for Paula's two year old. Paula has a job as a car*

131

mechanic and arms full of scars from the abscesses caused by injecting heroin.

'Methadone does your teeth in,' she told me. 'It's full of sugar.'

Paula said that the woman she robbed was disabled.

'But you couldn't tell. I think she had arthritis.'

Paula's partner in the crime was her ex-husband, who could be seen on the CCTV reversing at speed down the street and around the corner. He wasn't charged.


## JESUS

Many young women in here wear plastic rosary beads, in a variety of colours, around their neck or wrists. Jesus is very popular in Bronzefield and I understand why. If he was around, these are the people he'd be with. He'd be telling them that, contrary to what they'd been told or had learned, someone did actually love them, scars and all.


## JACKIE

Jackie goes home on Wednesday. She has told many of the women in 2C why I'm here and she has ordered them to like me for it. Every so often she calls out to check that I'm OK. She did this today.

'Not long now Jackie,' I said.

'No. Wednesday. Are you alright Lin?'

'I'm a bit down today Jack.'

'You know you can always come and talk to me. Don't be on your own like that. Come and have a chat.'

*I don't know why Jackie is in prison, I haven't asked and she's never said. But she has the tell-tale blackened and missing teeth. She's loud and raucous but her invitation to come and 'talk' is filled with concern for me. I hope she makes it on the outside. Jackie, like so many others, is someone I want to take home, wrap in a blanket and feed with homemade chicken soup.*

**March 29th 4:20 pm** I only have one more page of my 'Day One Christian Ministries' diary to turn over and I will be able to see the 'Going Home' page. At one minute into Sunday April 5th, I can turn the page. This page turning day is also Robbie's 54th birthday.

On my 60th birthday, while playing a gig at The King Arthur, he called me up to the stage. He sat me down on a throne he'd made from a wicker chair covered in purple velvet and surrounded by lights. With Aaron on keyboards and Robbie with no guitar, he sang to me, 'The First Time Ever I saw Your Face.' He'd been practising. Robbie then took my hand and danced with me. I felt like the most loved person on earth. And later Robbie told me how pleased he was that he'd been able to reach the high note in that song.

**March 29th After lock up** Two weeks and five days. Sometimes I believe that I'm creating some value in here, and then I get embarrassed being in the company of such a pompous, condescending arsehole.

## SUSAN

*March 30*[th] *Today I had a furtive chat with Susan Nicholls. She wrote her name and number on a small piece of paper which I folded and hid in my bra. Susan told me that during her trial for d o g theft, the owner of the beagle e x p l a i n e d how distressed he was at the theft of his dog, 'a member of the family'. A letter was p r o d u c e d from h i s children expressing their heartbreak at the loss of their pet. The judge described the letter as 'very touching'. He didn't ask why the RSPCA had been called so many times regarding the dog, which was permanently chained up in the garden and muzzled. The owner removed the muzzle to feed it and then put it back on again. Apparently it was muzzled because it continually chewed the fence, trying to escape. The 2006 Animal Welfare Act states that the person responsible for the animal must ensure the following:*

(a) its need for a suitable environment,

(b) its need for a suitable diet,

(c) its need to be able to exhibit normal behaviour patterns,

(d) any need it has to be housed with, or apart from, other animals, and

(e) its need to be protected from pain, suffering, injury and disease.

*Quite how bad the treatment of the animal needs to be before the RSPCA take any action I can't say, but clearly Susan Nicholls wasn't able to wait and find out.*

*What is rare in prison is to find someone who is serving a sentence for animal cruelty. Bronzefield however has had one. The woman served three months for killing a puppy with a knife. I've been told it was a long three months for her.*

*When I asked Susan if I could put her in my prison journal, she was suspicious but then agreed, with the proviso, 'I don't want any poor Susan stuff. I'd do five years to save that dog.'*

*I suspect that those who knew about the cruelty to the dog didn't have the courage to take action themselves. But they knew a woman who would.*

**March 31ˢᵗ** Bronzefield for me is a lesson, a lesson in patience. Waiting around is part of our punishment and it causes the heart to pound and the teeth to clench. I don't know why I find it so frustrating, after all, where else am I going to go? Another part of the punishment is the demand that we be in three places at the same time. If we fail to do this we will miss one of the following: our meal, our medication, our visit or an appointment, any of which will be our fault because we weren't where we were supposed to be when any of these were happening.

**March 31st After dinner** Paula has turned out to be a racist. She felt safe expressing her views to me and then I had to decide what to do. Should I give her enough rope to let her hang herself? Should I nail my colours to the mast? Or should I try to squeeze another cliché into this paragraph? My flag is now flying high and flapping in the wind.

**April 1st** Louise Hartley, VM4859, sent me an internal letter and a leaflet. The letter told me about her trial and the leaflet is to raise money for a Greek Animal Sanctuary. Both were returned to her with the explanation, 'No internal post is allowed.' Death of a thousand cuts.

**Paula** is desperately trying to back pedal and I have to say that I'm enjoying watching her legs spin so fast. This experience won't change her attitude of course, except perhaps to teach her not to assume that another white person will automatically share her views.

### JO
*Jo left today; big, cuddly Jo. A few days ago she decided that I was 'OK'.*

*'I like people like you, people who help animals and stuff,' she said. She then left my cell only to return a couple of minutes later carrying a photo of*

*her two children holding their Nan's small, shiny-eyed
dog.*

*'What kind of dog is that?' she asked me.*

*'Not sure exactly but it's some type of terrier.'*

*'You can tell it's healthy can't you?'*

*'Oh yes. I can see that he's loved,' I told her.
Jo seemed to want my approval.*

*I found out a few days ago that Jo is being
released soon and each morning since then I've said to
her, 'Not long now Jo.' Only today did I learn that Jo
can't make it on the outside; 'Institutionalised' is the
familiar t e r m  u s e d  by those familiar with everything
it means.*

*'I kept standing at shop doors waiting for
someone to unlock them,' one woman said as w e were
talking about Jo.*

*Each time I said to Jo, 'Not long now,' the
anticipation of freedom was mine, not hers. Two
days before her release Jo started shouting in the
dinner queue, throwing her plate across the floor. I
thought someone had upset her. Now I know. For Jo,
'freedom' was the knowledge that she was exchanging
the routine she knows, the safety of an indifferent
regime, for the danger of choice.*

**April 2<sup>nd</sup>** This morning at 9 am I have an
interview with probation to discuss my release on
HDC. It is now 9:06 and I'm locked in my cell with a
promise from Polly, a decent officer on duty, that she'll
come to get me when the probation officer arrives. Part

of my HDC process is to complete an 'Offending Chart'. The chart is divided into sections:

**a. How the offence was planned.**
**b. How the offence was carried out.**
**c. The effects on the victim.**
**d. The effects on me.**
**e. The effects on my family and friends.**
**f. My feelings and thoughts.**
**g. What percentage did I consider to?**
   **be my responsibility?**

For 'g' I have written '100%'. For 'c' I have written 'unsure'.

I'm passing the time completing the Suduko (elementary) in yesterday's Independent, while I try to control my blood pressure, which wasn't taken yesterday because I arrived for my medical appointment at 3:20 pm and by 4:30 pm I had given up and left. The experience of making the decision to leave for myself was worth the wait. Only someone who has never been in prison could be late for an appointment upon which our release hinges.

**April Fools' Day** someone put a notice on the board in the wing. It read:

*For £5 from your canteen account you can enjoy a*
*Day Trip to the coast. Sign up here:*
Seven people signed up.

138

**April 3rd Visitors** Two dogs came trotting into the wing this morning looking for drugs, tails wagging, running around. The white English women fussed and stroked while the Somali women kept far away and the black English women cursed, 'nasty'. I gave these dogs the love I can't give my Bob until April 17th.

I wander into clichés when I think of dogs. I hear 'bond' and 'love' and 'loyalty'. I find myself among that dreadful poetry. I battle with the banal, the trite. How can I say that which so many have tried to say and failed? He has no need for my forced and stilted courtesy; my dog is not polite company. And when good friends say I can call them anytime, 3 am if necessary, my dog is there at 3 am. And when I unexpectedly drop by and catch a whisper of the inconvenience, he is never inconvenienced. When I am forcing my inexplicable sadness to stay inside, to hide that which I cannot explain, my dog is there, not asking that I be sane, asking for nothing... but me, with all of my failings.

Two days ago we lost some people from 2C and their new replacements have arrived, carrying their attitude along with their clear plastic bags. This morning there was a loud argument and 2C feels oppressive and on edge. It's the pointlessness of it, the shouting, the rage just below the surface, the squabbling over a packet of crisps or scrap of food, the Oriental women pushed to the back of the queue, slyly. And it's the officers, indifferent to everything but the most outrageous. The battle to hang onto Lin is relentless.

**April 3<sup>rd</sup> After lunch** Just spoken to Robbie. Ten minutes earlier, outside probation had phoned him to organise my HDC. He also told me that my visit with Little John, Chris and Katy is arranged for the morning. A n d  n o w  the daffodils look even more glorious in my mind than they looked when I walked past them this morning.

I've written a letter to Rose. She has no one in this country, so now she has me.

**April 3<sup>rd.</sup> After dinner** Another argument, same people. Something went missing and someone was accused. The missing item was found under the owner's bunk.

Just as children can't wait to speak, to take their turn, neither can the English women, both young and not so young. They seem to be stuck at eleven. There is a theory that a trauma in early life causes us to be stuck at the age it happened but my mind can't go to that place today.

**April 4<sup>th</sup>** Ashleigh is seventeen today. Have a wonderful birthday my beautiful granddaughter.

**April 4<sup>th</sup> Breakfast** One of the keys to living in prison isn't learning the rules; it's learning how each

140

officer interprets those rules. This morning I wore jogging trousers a n d a pyjama top to queue for breakfast and the officer told me to change; pyjamas aren't allowed for breakfast. I think this is a reasonable rule, unsure why they have it, but reasonable. Yesterday pyjama tops *and* bottoms were allowed in the breakfast queue. In 3C the rules were fixed, except that Beverley liked loud music so this was allowed. On 2C loud music is discouraged and banned by some officers.

## THE BLACK PAW CLUB

Lewis Trust Dwellings, Dalston Lane, Hackney didn't allow tenants to keep dogs or cats in the fifties or sixties, when my family lived there. But when I brought home Sooty as a kitten, Dad, who made all the decisions, allowed me to keep him. My brother John and I used to be sent out to dig up soil for his washing-up bowl litter tray. This stayed on the balcony between the toilet and the kitchen.

Sooty lived with us for many years, hidden away like a refugee. He used to sleep on my bed and during Dad's alcoholic ravings, my fear was always that he'd hurt my cat. I felt safer, for myself and Sooty, if I could feel his warmth through the blankets.

There were three of us in the Black Paw Club, including Diane, but the third person has faded into my memory. Each week it was decided that we should put our pocket money into the old toffee tin with a picture of a grey fluffy kitten on it. My pocket money varied from zero to lots, depending upon how much Dad was drinking and the effect the drink had on his mood; a generous mood landed me half a crown, a foul one, zero. This money would then be saved to feed any starving animal we found. And one day the money was needed.

He was the biggest, blackest dog I had ever seen and we found him leaning up against the block of flats that held my number, 158. I knew nothing about dogs. I'd never known any and I'd never known anyone who'd owned one. Cats were fairly understandable. They are the Christines of the animal world. We opened our toffee tin and counted our money. There wasn't much, as the club had only been formed two weeks earlier and we'd already dug into it for some necessities: Black Jacks and Flying Saucers. There was just enough for a large tin of the cheapest dog food, which one of us went to buy while the others stayed with the dog. He didn't move, just remained leaning up against the wall. We told each other he was starving and so weak that he had to lean. We created a life story for him and then we fed him. That was as far as the Black Paw Club objectives went really. What we did with the starving animals after we'd saved them was further along than our years would allow. So I asked Mum.

'You have to take him to the police station,' she told us.

By then only Diane and I were around, the third member of the Black Paw Club having been called in for tea. But as Diane and I were the bedrock of all adventures, we would finish what we'd begun. Diane and I were allowed a lot of freedom, mainly because Mum was pre-occupied with survival and Diane's parents were certified insane since their breakdown, when her dad had been sacked from his job after being caught stealing. The shame took them both to the edge and tipped them over into a land of mutterings and unwashed bodies.

I remember the dog walking slowly as we tugged on the string we'd tied around his neck. We walked along Dalston Lane, past Ridley Road Market and around the corner to the police station. This was just down the road from Dalston Junction Station and almost opposite the undertakers that I used to run past with my head turned away. The dead were my biggest fear back then. I remember the police officer being very serious and kind and promising us that he would take care of the starving dog. He explained that he'd be taken around the back and put into a kennel after which he'd be sent to a dog's home. Pictures of armchairs and cushions came into my mind. I knew that he was telling the truth because he was a policeman and policemen don't lie; they're not allowed to.

Slowly the Black Paw Club faded and the toffee tin, with the picture of the grey fluffy kitten, was later used to keep shiny and sparkly things.

**April 4<sup>th</sup> 9:15 am** One of the women on remand in 2C was found not guilty in court yesterday. I wonder what happens now. Does she say, 'I'd like my time back please, hour for hour, minute for minute?'

How do we give her back the hours a n d days away from her children, the paddles in the sea? How do we rectify the lock ups and the pat-downs? I wonder if she is as angry for herself as I am for her.

**April 5<sup>th</sup>** A woman was attacked yesterday. I remember her from 3A. Ellie didn't like her. Today at 10:40 am Polly told me that I was moving to 2A. I believe these two things are connected but I have no way of finding out. I was given fifteen minutes to pack. I gave my beautiful flowers, sent to me by Robbie, to Diana, who'd been friendly and kind and never asked for a thing. Paula offered to help me carry my things; my books and letters are getting heavier with each day. I get so much post that one day a woman asked me, 'Are you famous?'

I packed everything into the plastic sacks and by 11:10 am I was standing on a chair in cell 26, Block 2A, scraping toothpaste off the walls. I decided not to sulk for a day this time but just get on with it, although I still believe my theory that this is Bronzefield's way of getting the prison cleaned.

By 11:30 Natasha, who is in a cell downstairs, had given me her spare clean bedding she was saving

144

in case next week's didn't appear. Eva, the classroom assistant with the orange flower, had given me her fan, which I use to dry my clothes, and a strange young woman with a cross eye, who works in servery, gave me an extra yoghurt. I soon realised that I recognised a few faces and this seems to be a friendlier wing. Of course there are always those who jump the food queue anytime they can. It's as though they have a plane to catch.

On a white envelope I have written, *'Freedom is a State of Mind'*. I have stuck this on the wall with toothpaste. Under it I have placed the picture of the dragonfly made for me by Ellie. The dragonfly is free.

This is the first time, despite all of my moves, that I haven't occupied Cell 17. I believe this is no coincidence; it is a code, a way of letting the officers know something about the prisoners. I have always been upstairs too. This also signifies something to them but what it is I don't know.

**April 5th Mid-afternoon** Out of my cell window the women from 2C, Khadra, Paula, Atash and others are out for 'association'. Many countries are represented in the April air today and at the G20 there is talk of a world free of nuclear weapons – a vast hope, a vast dream and now someone has spoken the words and sent the hope flying off for us all to see.

**April 5<sup>th</sup> After lock up** For one hour on Saturday and one hour on Sunday, the prisoners of Bronzefield can go outside for 'association'. We can associate with others in our block. There are blocks 1, 2 and 3 and each block has 4 wings, A, B, C, and D. Today I looked out of my window to see some familiar faces from 2C. I also saw Susan Nicholls, who is in 2B, the wing where the 'enhanced' prisoners stay. Susan walked around the triangle, which measures about 200 metres. Round and around she walked, getting her exercise. This triangle will be Susan's exercise for the next two years.

**Little John** When I remember leaving him I can only look in glimpses, peeking through my fingers. I bring this picture into my mind just to remind me that I have no right, ever, to be happy.

**April 6<sup>th</sup>** I am back with Iris for the rest of my sentence. I believe this is called 'doing hard time'. Today she snatched a worksheet out of my hands because she thought that a Romanian woman called Oana was looking at my answers. Oana is more than able to complete the work correctly.

**April 6<sup>th</sup> Dinner time** There is an over-current of aggression on 2A. The woman who attacked someone is in here, as is the mixed-race woman who always needed my seat or paper. She's teamed up with a tall, muscular, mixed-race woman and the aggression radiates from them. According to Natasha, there were two fights in 2A last week. Lizzie is here also and her bump is still so tiny she hardly looks pregnant. I have no menu again, as I've been moved. There are several of us with no menus, which means that we have to wait until everyone else has been given their food. Not a problem if those with menus come and join the line when they're called, but they don't. We have to wait; our dinner is what's left over and what's left over is always cold.

**April 7<sup>th</sup> Choices** Most mornings I have three choices: my blood pressure tablet, my breakfast along with my daily pack, half a pint of milk, 4 teabags, 4 sachets of sugar, 3 sachets of coffee and 2 sachets of jam or Gongyo. I haven't missed a Gongyo since I've been here and I usually manage breakfast. Today I missed my tablet because of the difficulty I have in splitting myself in two. 'Meds' were called at some time during breakfast while I was doing Gongyo.

**April 7<sup>th</sup> After dinner** I had my dinner, had a shower and  listened to a fight. The same person who had beaten up the other prisoner is continuing to travel around the block like a shark, taking chunks. The tall, muscular woman was animated and laughing. Like any system or machine, one dysfunctional part and it ceases to work.

Many women were gathered at the spur gates, screaming and shouting. I looked over the balcony outside my cell and resisted the urge to go down. I heard Josie's name mentioned. Possibly they're trying to take her to isolation, which was murmured today. But it's not Josie who disturbs me. She's clearly unwell. No, it's the exhilaration and delight with which violence is greeted. Just under the surface is the animal in all of us.

As I do Gongyo there's screaming and shouting around me, women kicking off for being locked up early. Three or four at a time, they let us out to fill our flasks for the night. By the urn a woman with scars on her face asked me if I was OK. I must have looked scared. She sounded very concerned for me and it touched my heart, as small kindnesses so easily do in this place. We've all been locked in our cells now.


**April 8<sup>th.</sup> Before breakfast** I can hear the keys. I can hear the shouting. But no one has come to unlock my cell. Thoughts of having been forgotten come to me. Don't panic. I've been locked up for fifteen hours now.

Woke up crying this morning and chanted again for peace in here and peace for Josie. Eight days to go and I've heard nothing about my release. Perhaps it's like a visit; one hour before it's due we're told it's going to happen.

148

Yesterday once again, Iris mentioned Buddhism. I told her that I was a Buddhist when I first went into her class. I have no idea why I did this except I fell into the classic trap of thinking that, as she had a slightly 'new age' feel about her, the crystals and yoga type, she may be interested. She now mentions Buddhism regularly. During lunch I quickly finished reading 'The Buddha, Geoff and Me' for the second time so that I could give it to her.

**April 8<sup>th</sup> After lunch** Last night four prisoners attacked a male officer; that's what the noise was, the shouting, the jubilation that violence brings. I hope he's not hurt too badly. Is there a point in prison at which a prisoner begins to see an injured officer as a victory? How long would I have to be in here before that happens?

**April 8<sup>th</sup> Before dinner** The lovely Diana has been moved onto 2A. We had a cuddle. It was like seeing an old friend, finding a comfy jumper. Lovely, smiley, friendly Diana. Six feet tall with a haircut that would be considered funky if it hadn't been an accident. Diana is here and I am happy.

**April 9<sup>th</sup> Class** All the women in here want to earn certificates. There are certificates for IT, massage, cleaning. Women, who didn't go to school or weren't sent to school, eagerly aspire for the certificates, for recognition. Today Natasha showed me her certificate for IT.

'I want to show Mum what I've done,' she said, holding the certificate at arm's length. 'I want to show her that I'm not just a druggie. I can do stuff.'

As Bronzefield is run for profit, having a teacher inmate should please the shareholders. Why pay for a supply teacher when Judge Simpton has supplied one for them free of charge. There's some part of me that wants a shareholder's house to be burgled and the burglar sent to a private prison. This system does, after all, rely on crime for their profits to continue. They could always use the profits from their shares to replace their stolen property.

**April 10th** Four days Easter holiday or four days during which nothing happens towards my release, depends which way it's looked at, from the door or the window. Our lives bounce off each other, sometimes like a bubble off a curtain and sometimes like a cricket ball in the face. Whether my life has been a bubble or a ball I don't know. Some people, in here and on the outside, are people I just shy away from. Like a chained and snarling dog, I'm never quite sure how long their chain is.

I read my guidance each day and never fail to feel better about myself, even if it's just for the moments I'm reading. Today Nichiren assured me that I don't have to be clever or perfect. All I have to do is chant. We don't throw away something precious

150

just because the container that holds it is flawed or damaged.

Thank you Nichiren.

**Yvonne** seems different, softer, more open. She told me yesterday that she'd threatened to 'bang someone out'. Then she said, 'I don't want to do it because I feel bad afterwards but I just need to be left alone when I'm feeling like that.'

We talked about 'time out', the system that Solomon's teacher uses for him.

'That's exactly what I need but they just stay in my face. If only they'd let me be on my own for a while, I'll come round,' Yvonne said. 'That's all I need.'

If prisons were really serious about suicide prevention they wouldn't simply monitor the obvious: razors and shoelaces. They wouldn't give us plastic bags to put over our heads and cells over a twenty foot drop onto concrete. But if prisoners were really serious about suicide we'd use what we're given: plastic bags and twenty foot drops onto concrete.

Little John has written to tell me that according to their website, Bronzefield has Level 4 Healthcare, the highest achievable. So Level 2 must mean that sore throats are treated with Jeyes Fluid.

The heating has now been turned off until October. There's a lot of complaining about the cold. Load of softies. They just don't make criminals like they used to.

**April 11<sup>th</sup> After lunch** Last night I was so hungry I opened all of my sachets of sugar and ate them. So far today I have saved an egg from breakfast and an extra orange from lunch. Dinner on Friday, Saturday and Sunday is iceberg lettuce, half a tomato cut in two and some slices of cucumber. Along with this, those who have a menu, have what they had chosen from the week before: egg, tuna or peanut butter. Those without a menu wait to see what is left. Sometimes I take the roll to give to another prisoner, sometimes I don't. I gave it to Diana yesterday before Christine could ask.

Christine has been moved onto 2A to separate her from the sluggish laundry woman with whom she had been fighting. Perhaps she had to wait three days for her laundry also. Now why didn't I think of that? Grab that slow laundry woman by the hair and throw her on the floor, screaming and scratching.

Today I sat downstairs after dinner and a small, thin woman began chatting to me. She asked why I was in here and I told her. Then she said, 'Where's the dog now?'

'I can't tell you that,' I said.

'Why? Do you think I'm going to tell someone?' she said, staring straight at me.

The atmosphere chilled. I felt her trying to drag me into something but I didn't know what. Did she want to know the whereabouts of Hess so that she could have some kind of hold over me? Did she just want an argument or a fight?

152

'Only my partner and the person who has the dog know where he is. Even my family doesn't have the address,' I said.

I left her sitting at the table and went up to my cell. I felt unnerved but couldn't tell anyone in case it all blew up.


**April 11<sup>th</sup> Before dinner** I don't know if it's incompetence or deliberate cruelty. Tomorrow Robbie, Bobby and Nig were coming for a visit. Today I phoned Robbie. He's been told that the visit he had been trying to arrange isn't going to happen because it's a bank holiday. My HDC, due in five and a half days, has yet to be confirmed. Now I understand the screams in the night, the door pounding, the TV smashing, the cell trashing, the officer on the floor in a ball. I believe they may be too incompetent to be deliberately cruel; that would need some organization. Four days in a cell, no visit, no idea what's happening, no one to ask, no one to ignore my questions.

I have decided that if my HDC goes one hour past April 17<sup>th</sup> I'll withdraw my application for it. This means I'll be released on May 14<sup>th</sup> with no tag. I'll *give* them a month but they won't *take* a fucking minute from me!

I am telling myself that it is now five weeks and one day until my release but I have just realised that, as well as my HDC being at the discretion of the prison, so is my eighteen day early release of May

153

14$^{th}$. Therefore I must get it into my head that my release date is June 1$^{st}$. I wonder if this is actually anything to do with me at all. Is this a way of getting me to say where Hess is or is it simply a beige file in a metal filing cabinet that was going to be looked at but the train was late.

## April 12$^{th}$ Afternoon
## My letter to the Prison Governor.

*I work as a classroom assistant in an ESOL class and, as a retired teacher, have on occasions been given responsibility for teaching the class when the prison is a teacher short. I enjoy my job very much. I am in prison because I refuse to return an elderly mongrel dog that I had been looking after. However, I have broken the law and have no complaints about being punished for it. This is my first offence and I have been given an HDC date of April 17$^{th}$ 2009. I am 60 years old. So why do I feel the need to write to you?*

*Each Saturday I am given a VO which I immediately complete and post in a stamped envelope. One hour before a visit I am given a slip to tell me the visit is going to happen. Last Saturday, April 4$^{th}$, I followed the same routine. Yesterday April 11$^{th}$, I learned from my partner that the prison was unable to arrange the visit for April 12$^{th}$ because it is a bank holiday.*

*Only those who have never been in prison could fail to understand how devastating this is. My partner* $^{h}$

154

received his VO on his return from work on *April 8th*, four days after it was posted with a *1st* class stamp. He phoned on the *9th* to book the visit. He received no reply, as is normal with the Bronzefield system. When he finally did manage to speak with someone he was told that a visit wasn't possible because of the bank holiday.

## HDC

I have an HDC date of April *17th*. I have sent a VO for a visit on the *18th* or *19th* as I have had no notification to let me know the status of my HDC. I am unsure if any of this is due to incompetence, deliberate cruelty or simply because the people dealing with it don't care.

But what has happened to me is this: I have gone from being a 'model prisoner', *quietly getting on* with doing her time, to one crying with frustration. I can now understand why cells are trashed, doors pounded and why women yell and scream in the middle of the night. I am fortunate enough to be articulate and literate but for those who aren't it must be hell.

I have just read in the paper that violent attacks in prison are on the increase. I don't believe there is **ever** an excuse for violence but I do understand how a system, which appears to not be answerable for its actions, can push a person's frustration to the surface. I feel that the system in Bronzefield does nothing to protect its officers or prisoners. When people feel helpless and believe they're not being listened to, the result is frustration and for some, violence.

I realise that it's too late to do anything about my visit; that time has passed. However, if anything can be done so that another prisoner doesn't miss a precious visit because it happens to be a bank holiday, then hopefully this letter will help.

Regards

### THE LOVELY DIANA

The lovely Diana has been on hard drugs since she was fifteen. She has a thirteen year old son who she handed over to her mum when he was two because she knew this was the best thing for him. Diana had been a prostitute but when she fell in love with her current boyfriend, she stopped working the streets.

'It's the only time I've been faithful,' she told me.

Diana was kicked out of rehab for having sex with another inmate. She'd almost completed her time there.

'I told them I'd give up drugs. I didn't tell them I'd give up shagging,' she said.

Diana is now on 10ml of methadone and hopes to be clean by the time she leaves. She has been in prison before for shoplifting. Diana is bright, open, self-aware big-hearted and wonderful. She hasn't seen her son for the three and a half months she's been here and she's been told that he's 'kicking against authority'. She arranged a visit for him today that would allow her to talk to him as she's worried he's going to get into *trouble. Her visit, just like mine, didn't go ahead because it is a bank holiday.*

*I have an urge to write to her son and tell him about his mum. Naive probably but this is what I want to do, to tell a thirteen year old how great his mum is, how proud she is of him, how much she loves him.*

*Diana's younger sister is at university studying dentistry.*

*'I think I helped her. She looked at me and realised that my life is not what she wanted,' she told me.*

If I don't get anything else out of prison, I've met the lovely Diana and that's enough.

**April 13<sup>th</sup> Breakfast** My back really hurts again today. I can barely walk. Duffy gave me her tube of Deep Heat to use. She noticed I was in pain. I handed an officer my rather long-winded and pompous letter to the Governor. Strangely, he took it immediately to the officer's station.

**April 13<sup>th</sup> 9.15 am** Two officers have just searched my cell, thirty minutes after I handed them my letter to the Prison Governor. Very polite as always, they patted me down and then I stood outside the door until they had finished. When they called me back in one of them was holding my tweezers.

'You can't keep these. They have to be in your 'greens.'

Our 'greens' are the files on each prisoner which are kept on the wing. I explained that my cell had been searched before and that the officer allowed me to keep my tweezers.

'At my age you get a bit whiskery,' I joked. They laughed at my feeble humour and walked off with my tweezers, leaving me to remake my bed and tidy my cell. My problem now is that during my dark times, when I have reached the end, I won't have anything with which to pluck myself to death.

I went to visit Diana and Clare in their double cell. In there were two giggly young girls. Diana thought they were being disrespectful towards me so she threw them out. Diana and I have had the same thought. She would like her son to be mentored by one of my sons. Will this all be forgotten when we get our lives back?


**April 14<sup>th</sup> Early morning** A doctor's appointment has been pushed under my door. It's for 16:20 today. How will I get my dinner?

I have stopped marking off the days on my calendar and I'm telling myself that this uncertainty is part of the punishment; it's easier that way.

I mentioned to Iris last week that I may be released on the 17<sup>th</sup>.

'Well that's something we need to know. We have to make arrangements,' she said.

I don't think she means to book me a taxi.


**April 14<sup>th</sup> After dinner** There's a civilian employee who walks around the prison listening to our concerns and then telling us why he can't help. I explained about my HDC. He gave me his sympathetic face and explained that HDC 'is a privilege not a right' so they have their own time scale.

Robbie said that he wished they didn't have HDC or eighteen day early release at all. A release date should be a release date but I don't think it would work as they'd have nothing with which to torment us.

One of the Chinese women asked me why she's still in prison when her sentence ended ten days ago. Lots of the foreign national women ask me questions to which I have no answers. Shrugging is becoming automatic now. I want to say, 'Sorry but I don't know the Cantonese for "inept" and "disarray."'

I've realised that many of the students are frightened of Iris. But rudeness is just her manner, perhaps the way she was parented. She was even rude to Joe last week when he popped his head around the door to ask a question. She's n e v e r rude to Pamela though, the other ESOL teacher. Last week Khadra said to me, 'In my religion Mohammed says it's not good to make people afraid.'

'Yes, in my religion too,' I told her.

**April 15th Before unlock** My pens are running out and I can't order any more until next week, which means I won't get them until Thursday 23rd. Last night I received no post, for the f i r s t  t i m e since I've been here. I also received no Independent, for the fifth time, despite Robbie paying for me to receive them. I wonder where they go.

**Prison Notice:**
*'Don't count the days. Make the days count.'*
*Hmm...*
A problem shared is a problem halved.
It takes more muscles to frown than it does to smile. You can lead a horse to water but you can't make it surf.

If a cliché was clothing, it would be a beige cardigan

**April 15th After lunch** My application enquiry regarding my HDC has been answered. Despite outside probation calling Robbie on April 2nd, as of April 14th they have failed to complete my home probation report so my 'board can't sit'. I may now withdraw my application for HDC as it can take another two weeks and I can go home with no tag in four weeks. I'm crying now but at least I know. Perhaps this will relieve my back; it feels as locked in as the rest of me.

Prison seems to be featuring more and more in Iris' lessons and she appears not to notice the tears.

But then again she is into 'self-help' books not 'help-others' books. Today the students were given the words 'recession' and 'repossession' to put into their little red vocabulary books. With the latter Iris went into detail, adding 'bailiff' to the list and taking the opportunity to explain how some women, while in prison, have their homes 'repossessed' because they are unable to pay the 'mortgage' whereby the 'bailiffs' come in to remove their furniture.

'Do you know anyone this has happened to Lin?'

'Unfortunately not Iris. Sorry.

**April 16<sup>th</sup>** It's commonly said that the body can heal itself and I think the mind has the capacity to do this also. The damage caused by finding out that I won't be going home tomorrow, as I'd been led to believe since I first arrived, is repairing itself. In its place I am putting reasons to stay and take my eighteen day early release. I want to get to know Diana better. She popped in for a cup of tea yesterday; yes, just like home.

**April 16<sup>th</sup> Lunchtime** I've been given an Alpha appointment, which means I have to see the shrink again. I'm going to talk to her about the regime in here that appears to be sending even sane people slightly mad. Lizzie believes that everything is part of our punishment, from the electric shocks our cell doors never fail to deliver, to the lack of information we are given.

**April 16<sup>th</sup> Dinner time** Tonight on the phone I gave Robbie the job of deciding for me whether I should stay here until mid-May or go home when my HDC finally comes through. He paused for a few moments and then said, 'I want you to come home free, not walking around with something around your ankle. I want to take you out for dinner. I want you free, totally free.'

The relief of not having to make this decision made me sob but Robbie knew why I was crying. Now I can't stop smiling at the thought that I can see my freedom. I don't have to catch glimpses of it hidden behind tea-ringed papers and suited people speaking of mortgage rates, while shuffling my life into a pile of other lives.

### PAM AND THE RSPCA

I've finally received the email from Pam, an RSPCA inspector, who saw mine and Robbie's tirade against her organisation on the website Robbie has setup. Her story is harsh and frustrating and I felt ashamed as I read it:

*'It really grieves me to read your letter. For several reasons: for the dog, for Lin, and for the RSPCA (the first 2 for obvious reasons). The third one upsets me because I work for the RSPCA. I did it*

162

voluntarily for about 18 years and have been employed for about the same length of time - so hopefully, you will see that this wasn't just a job to me - it was a vocation. I take it personally if we have let an animal down. It is as though I have let it down myself. BUT, I don't know the circumstances of the neglect. I know we are not perfect but I do wonder if people out there realise what our Inspectors are up against, ie more calls (allegations of cruelty) than one person per town can cope with. Aborted house visits - no-one in. Having to return several times. So much time going to waste. Can't plan a route - priorities of need don't allow for this. In the middle of one call, - not me, but our local Inspector) - get another call for a rescue (10 hours this week spent trying to catch a goose with a crossbow in its back - but it can still fly!!!)

Inspector responds to complaint about a limping puppy. Collects it, takes it to a vet, picks it up again after x-rays and repair, tries to find accommodation (animal centre) - have to travel 20 miles to an animal home with a kennel space) - 20 miles back - over half a day gone. All very time consuming. Lesser (non-life and death) calls have to wait until tomorrow. Tomorrow brings more urgent complaints. Some calls have to be put back again. Do the public realise that we have one Inspector per town and if that one person is off sick or on holiday, etc. then there is one Inspector for two towns?

**If an animal has no physical signs of abuse, then we cannot get a vet to support our case in**

163

*court. All our prosecutions have to be backed up by a vet - otherwise we won't win in court and an animal that may have been seized will be ordered to be returned to the owner. That's the law and we cannot go against it.*

*We are classed as the 4th emergency service - by the public, whose expectation has made us too big for our own boots - as a charity we cannot meet those expectations. To suggest withdrawing funds will only make matters worse, not better. There will be no-one to take over where we lack (and I know we do) - if we have to have charities to help children or hospices or kidney machines, etc. etc. - there is no chance that the government will step in to help animals. I, too, support the Dogs Trust - but they only help canines. I support the Horse Welfare - but they only help equines, the Cat Protection - but they only help felines. Few of these charities have put themselves in the unenviable and costly position of investigating cruelty and taking people to court. That, and boarding these seized animals which we cannot re-home until months down the line, when a court has acted in our favour, costs us a six figure sum each year.*

*Despite our failings, the RSPCA is still the charity for me because we try to respond to all creatures. In the last few weeks our branch with no animal centre has rescued 50 rabbits, 20 mice, 2 budgies, 4 cockatiels, 2 soft-shelled turtles, 6 ponies, a goat, 15 cats, 7 dogs, 5 ducks plus various wild animals. I am not perfect - just exhausted,*

164

*mentally and physically. I have no answers and no facilities to take in all the animals that people cannot keep because: they have lost their houses, a baby is allergic, they can't afford vet's fees, a couple has split up, etc. It is mental torture not being able to do what we want to do for all these animals, and what people expect us to do. I give out telephone numbers of other organisations, praying for a miracle that they might have homed an animal and therefore have a space for another, knowing in my heart of hearts that they, too, are full. Which other charities have the manpower, training and financial back-up to respond to the flood disasters like the RSPCA did in 2007? But again, whilst over 30 Inspectors out of a total of 300 in the whole of England and Wales, were redeployed to other areas, that left gaps in their own towns . . . . . . . . . and so it goes on. They can't be in two places at once. These are not excuses - just explanations. Hope perhaps you may understand a little why we have so many shortcomings . . . . . . . . . . . . . . And wanted to say sorry (and thanks) to Lin and hope dog is now safe and happy.'*

When I read this I knew I was reading this woman's heart and I felt slightly ashamed that I had hurt her feelings. It isn't the individual, the people like Pam; it's the faceless organisation, the roll of barbed wire and red tape in which Pam is tangled, each move resulting in more tears and rips. Pam does a job I could

165

never do and, like all those involved in the rescue of animals, she is doing our dirty work for us.

Her confirmation that no vet will support a case of animal cruelty, unless there are physical signs of abuse, has brought home to me the hopelessness of my case in any court. We can drive an animal mad. We can leave it alone for days or weeks. We can do with it as we wish. As long as what we do to it doesn't show.

### THE SEARCH FOR HESS

*'60 year old retired teacher in court for dog theft,'* is a novel news story as is:

*'60 year old retired teacher sent to prison for Contempt of Court.'* Or even:

*'Cancer patient has much loved dog stolen! Have you seen this dog?'*

My appearances in court were never reported in our local papers, papers that run stories on stolen bicycles and unlicenced televisions. Veronica never went to the papers to tell her story and ask for help in finding Hess. If she had then people could have been looking. Each day, throughout the past twenty months, I have half expected to open a local paper and see a picture of Veronica holding a vacant lead and a crumpled hankie. It still puzzles me why she didn't do this.

At my final crown court appearance before being sent to prison, Judge Simpton warned us about

166

seeking 'publicity', threatening that, should the person who has Hess be found, they would be prosecuted for handling stolen goods. Robbie and I had made the decision not to go to the papers, despite many people telling us that we should. Our priority was always to protect the whereabouts of Hess, to keep him safe. But something about Judge Simpton's warning has always b a f f l e d me. Why would he discourage us from doing something that may help in the police's search for Hess? Why did he not want the story to be publicised?

**April 17<sup>th</sup>** I'm always happy to help, so when the young girl with a ridiculously flat, stony white stomach and bare midriff asked, 'Can you get me a razor? I'm on the card,' I agreed to do so, having no idea why she couldn't get a razor or what 'on the card' actually means.

In order to get a razor (or nail clippers or tweezers) we have to hand in our ID until we return the item. There are no nail clippers on the wing and haven't been for some time. My toenails are now very long and uncomfortable. So, on behalf of the girl, I asked the officer for a razor and he took my ID, only to return and tell me there would be no razors available until tomorrow. The young girl returned to my cell to collect the razor and I told her what the officer had said.

'What does "on the card" mean?' I asked her. She showed me her arms, sliced and scarred.

167

'But I won't do that. I'm happy at the moment,' she promised.

'Please don't do that to yourself. Why do you do that?'

'I won't go into it now but I won't do it. I promise. You can come into the bathroom with me if you like.'

The razor seemed to mean more to her than her own skin. Why are smooth legs more important to her than her lovely rosebud arms?

Today I have to tell her that I won't get the razor. I want to write, 'in case she cuts herself' and this is of course on my mind. But so is the issue of a warning for breaking the rules and too many warnings could mean lost privileges and a possible delay in my release. I want to believe that my priority is this young woman's safety but I'm not sure it is.

Yesterday I had an appointment to see the prison shrink for the second time since being here. I asked her how much say she had in the running of the prison. I went over the withholding of information about visits and HDC dates and the effect this has on the mind. I told her how Lizzie now believes that the prisoners are deliberately being given electric shocks through the cell doors.

'We have no say at all,' she told me. 'But maybe someone on the outside can let people know. They need to know. Yes, prisoners have a TV in their room but it doesn't mean anything. There's so much wrong in here. It's not about TVs.'

I noticed that she called the cells 'rooms' as though that made them sound less punitive. But they're supposed to be punitive; it's a prison. I wonder if they are told to refer to them as 'rooms' during their training sessions. Perhaps we should call being in prison 'a period of leave'. Much more benign. She then told me I should go home as soon as possible.

'Even two weeks later than you were told is still two weeks earlier than May 14th,' she said.

She is now going to phone the probation officer to ask her to come to speak to me. She is trying so hard and I feel as though I'm letting this woman down by cancelling my HDC but I feel so much better now that decision has been made. Just having the power to reject their offer gives me freedom. Fuck them and fuck their HDC!!

**April 17<sup>th</sup> Lunchtime** Iris was on good form this morning with more of the, 'How can we fit "prison" and "court" into as many sentences as possible?' The women have begun to search for the humour in Iris' cruelty and this immediately dilutes it. As I said to Zhara, 'We'll be out of prison one day. Iris will always be in prison.'

Zhara is three and a half months pregnant and quite unwell. The doctor gave her a note excusing her from the afternoon sessions in Education but Iris ignored the note and told Zhara that she had to attend. I've told her that I'll help her with a complaint if she

169

wishes but both Zhara and I know that nothing will be done. The complaint will be given a cursory once over and then it will be explained to her why their 'hands are tied'. That expression again. The sales of rope must be booming, recession or no recession.

**April 17<sup>th</sup> Afternoon** It's Friday afternoon so no work and no courses. Two women from probation have just visited me. It is odd to have people standing. I asked them both to sit down but they declined. Must be a rule. They looked and sounded concerned about the withdrawal of my HDC. They said that they'd had my outside probation report since Monday April 13th and that they were just starting my paperwork in time for Wednesday's board sitting. I could be out on Thursday or Friday.

If I hadn't spoken with Robbie yesterday I may have gone for this; the aroma of freedom crawled up my nose. In a few days I could be rocking with the tides or rocking in my man's arms. I asked them why everything is left until the last minute and they explained that a prisoner's release is dependent upon their behaviour and a prisoner may misbehave up until the last minute. I've heard of women walking out of the prison gates, only to be immediately brought back in again.

I have cleaned and rearranged my cell. My altar, or Butsudan to use the correct term, minus my Gohonzon, bell, incense and greenery, now sits next to the television. Leaning against the back wall is my dragonfly picture from Ellie and above it my white envelope stuck on with my own sticky, blue, non-drying toothpaste. May 14<sup>th</sup> here I come!

**April 17<sup>th</sup> After dinner** Officer Polly is on the spur today; quiet, firm, no nonsense, professional and fair, all that can be asked of an officer. Polly always makes a point of asking me how I am and it feels as though she really wants to know. That's an immense thing in here. Small kindnesses look huge to me. I feel safe with Polly.

Lizzie, Diana, Natasha and Duffy, these are the four people in 2A who I would go to for help. I wouldn't show my weakness to anyone else.

There was a film starring John Belushi, I can't remember the name, in which he was explaining to a friend from the countryside how to survive in a city. He said, 'When you're in the city, don't ever speak to anyone because they'll think you need help and they'll kill you.'

**April 17<sup>th</sup> After lock up** It had to happen. Even though my eye flap was closed, a male officer, checking that I was still in my cell and hadn't escaped by sliding under the door, caught me on the loo having a poo. The mortification I have been trying to avoid turned out to be more of an 'oh bugger!' moment. How do women manage to poo in front of each other when they share a cell? I find it

171

almost impossible to go when I'm staying in a strange place, even in the privacy of the pale blue tiled bathroom with the dolphin bath mat.

**April 18<sup>th</sup>** I have been measuring out my toothpaste so that it lasted until yesterday, my supposed-to-be release day. The prison no longer gives it out so I'll have to order it on my canteen on Thursday. I still have enough for a couple of days then I'll have to use salt, just as we did when we were kids in Hackney. Toothpaste was for the kids who had a garden and a bike and a dad who came home on paydays. Each Thursday evening, thirty minutes after the key didn't turn, I would be sent to The Lord Stanley to collect some of dad's wages before they went across the bar to stop him from being friendless. Making people happy made dad happy; that's how his mind worked. Dad needed people's happiness. And twice a year he made sure that we had ours. In the summer we were squeezed into a caravan with its grey blankets, crawling with earwigs, stuffed and stored in the musty cupboards. This was our happy time; Dad insisted.

We would be walked along the sea wall with dad taking huge breaths and shouting, 'Breathe deep. Get the shit out your lungs!' Mum would be about ten yards behind carrying jumpers, towels and anything else we may need for an English summer holiday.

And Christmas, one month after the annual building trade lay-off, where dad laboured for any firm that would take him, we had to be happy because

172

children are happy at Christmas; it's a rule. So for months before, dad would buy a weekly tin of pears, a Christmas pudding, a box of crackers that we called bonbons, and store them at the top of the cupboard in their bedroom. I think dad believed that these times made up for the drunken nights and the Thursday waiting. And to me they did. Dad did what he was able to do with the life he'd been given and each day that I live I see more of myself in him. It's easy to blame others for our suffering, for our reason not to love; it's easy and it's the coward's way.

Had a chat with Lizzie today and I can't help comparing her crime to Stev's attack on Alison, Robbie's sister. Stev beat her while she lay in bed next to their two year old son. I believe the charges ended up as common assault. His punishment for damaging her car was more severe than the one he received for damaging her. Does it now really just come down to how easy it is to get a conviction, how much work needs to be done for a guilty verdict? If so, we're living in very scary times.

**April 19<sup>th</sup>** Visit day. I count my time in visits now; four more and I go home. The sun is shining and there's a young woman outside my window. She's wearing blue shorts and a yellow T-shirt and she's bending over, shiny hair hanging d o w n , picking and gathering dandelions. She's not weeding; she's picking beautiful flowers to place in a polystyrene cup to brighten her cell.

173

What should I do about Iris' bullying? Bronzefield has a 'zero tolerance' policy towards bullying. Of course it does; I expect it has a policy for everything. But it only covers bullying by the prisoners. What do we do about bullying by the staff? Page ten of their brochure states what they consider bullying to be.

Under the heading:

**'Respect for each other. Support and protect the victim. Challenge the bully,'** *it* says:

*Being made to feel unwelcome, ignoring*
*'Borrowing' articles*
*Not being allowed to join in*
*Threats*
*Name calling*
*Queue jumping*

It goes on to give two phone numbers, one for 'Bullyline' and the other for 'The Samaritans'. Iris does none of those things listed but I feel that I need to do something, tell someone. How can I 'challenge' her? How can I 'support and protect the victim?' Most of the women in the ESOL class are on remand. In our system therefore they're still innocent because no one has yet to find them guilty. So Iris is not only bullying the women, she's bullying innocent women.

174

**April 19<sup>th</sup> After dinner** I've just had my visit from Robbie, Bobby and Nig. It's so strange to have normality and some reminders of my life and who I am. I hear myself talking at breakneck speed, trying to get it all out in an hour; the questions, the answers, no small talk, no weather, no family tiffs, none of the things that litter my life outside, each word now vital, each sentence sketching my life for me, as it was and as it soon will be again. Three more visits and then home.

**April 20<sup>th</sup> Observation** When we leave our cell we usually return to find it locked, unless we've been given a key which allows us to lock it ourselves. This isn't the main security lock, just one for our own peace of mind. Most people don't have these keys because previous prisoners haven't bothered to return them when they've been moved or released. When a prisoner finds herself locked out of her cell there are generally two methods for getting it unlocked? The first is to ask an officer and then wait for it to be done. The second is to swear, shout and kick the door repeatedly. The speed at which it is opened is not relative to the method used.

Mai Chan arrived in class today. She's from Malaysia and is quite fluent in English, which she learned by watching British television channels. This afternoon I watched her as she did an odd hair pulling and twisting massage on another woman, in order to relieve the woman's headache. I asked her if she did 'backs'. She then gave me the most wonderfully painful back massage, digging her thumbs into my pelvis. My back is now much easier and she's promised to do it again tomorrow.

In Bronzefield all pain is treated with Paracetemol.

*'My back hurts.'*

'Here's some Paracetemol.'

*'My head hurts.'*

'Here's some Paracetemol.'

*'My heart hurts because I haven't seen my children for three months and each time I speak to them on the phone my little girl cries and says, "Mummy, when are you coming home?"'*

'Here's some Paracetemol.'


**April 21st** Another nurse's appointment today, another no-show.


**April 21st After dinner** I have just spent two and a half hours with Iris writing a lesson plan for a two and a half hour lesson that I'm taking tomorrow while she's absent. Not enough that I'm in prison, locked away from my family, searched, ordered around, I now have to write bloody lesson plans! The lesson will be covering 'Directions' and 'Polite Requests'. Iris has insisted that the lesson focus on prison but I won't be doing this. What can she do, lock me up. This is a rhetorical question and I refuse to use a question mark.

I wonder if they have Ofsted in prison classes and if so, do they do what many schools do, give the really naughty pupils a day at home so they won't disrupt the class during inspection.

Not much shocks me unfortunately but the email I've just received from Robbie did. A detective sergeant no less, is threatening to arrest him unless he tells them where Hess is. Obviously the crime rate in Somerset must have plummeted, leaving them time to pursue the more heinous crimes. Robbie has always insisted that Veronica 'knows someone' and now I believe he may be right. Who is the important one, me or Veronica? Is it someone on her side or someone I have angered? Whoever it is, it appears that my prison sentence isn't enough for them. Perhaps the further this is taken, the more likely it will be that someone will begin to ask questions. Perhaps that's why Judge Simpton warned us about going to the media. I feel so angry for all those victims of crime who have been ignored by slightly disinterested police officers who simply 'don't have the manpower'

**April 22<sup>nd</sup> Early morning**   Robbie's email has really shaken me up. Will this never end or do we have to wait until Hess dies? I would rather have him put to sleep than return him to that life. I'd never rest knowing he was being left for days while Veronica was visiting Adam in his flat. Never once has Adam attended court with her. And I wonder if she has ever questioned this or even thought about it.

I must try to speak with Robbie this morning. As soon as they unlock my cell I'll phone him. I'm searching for some guidance, something to help me with the fear in my stomach.

*'Justice is like the sun. A society that lacks justice is shrouded in darkness. No one can stop the sun from rising. No cloud can hide the rays of the sun indefinitely. "Opening the eyes" means causing those hearts steeped in darkness to recognize the rising sun of justice.'*
**Daisaku Ikeda.**

Thank you Sensei.

### CHARLOTTE

*Charlotte has just completed a five day detox.*

*'I couldn't be arsed to do it the slow way so I planned it myself and signed the paper: 30ml, 25ml, 20ml, 10ml, 5ml, nothing.'*

*At the age of six Charlotte was raped by her father for the first time and she cut her arms to stop the pain. Now her arms are sliced and scarred with a thousand rapes. Charlotte was eleven when her father made her pregnant.*

*'I had an abortion. I don't really believe in them but I had to have one,' she explained, as though I might judge her for this.*

178

*Later Charlotte had surgery to repair the damage. What couldn't be repaired was removed. She has been living on the streets for ten years. One night Charlotte was woken up by a man who was trying to put his penis in her mouth so she stabbed and wounded him with the knife she always carried with her for protection. Charlotte was given two years.*

**April 22<sup>nd</sup>** There is now an elderly, very odd looking woman in 2A. She is tall, thin and wears leggings which emphasise her extremely bowed legs. Her tongue appears to be too large for her mouth and it lolls about. She has no teeth with which to keep it in check. I want to talk to her because we have just been given our post and she had none. Twice she said, 'I think my post went to Block One,' and twice the officer ignored her and then simply walked out. This woman looked lost and she's made me cry. Why is she in prison? Why isn't someone caring for her, giving her healthy food, talking to her, sending her letters? Where is her family? I'm going downstairs to give her some teabags and coffee. At times like these I would gladly swap my skin for that of a rhino. Perhaps I need to find Iris' bubble and climb inside.

**Phone call to Robbie** According to Robbie this morning, the detective sergeant told him that he'd use everything at his disposal, 'including arrest' (Robbie and others) and 'surveillance'. Aren't we important?

## LYNN AND THE LOVELY DIANA

*The old woman's name is Lynn. Diana found me crying and was worried. She gave me a cuddle. She has already said hello to Lynn and we both agreed that she shouldn't be in prison.*

*'She's clearly not well. She shouldn't be in here,' I said, stating what should be obvious.*

*'I know. She should be at home with people looking after her. My friend gave her a bra,' Diana told me.*

*I should have known that D i a n a would be the one to speak to her first. Some of the younger girls were making remarks about her and mimicking her big, uncontrollable tongue. I was angry at them.*

*'Prison has made them like that,' Diana said in their defence, showing me her compassion, even for those hardened to the injustice of imprisoning an old, sick woman. Diana puts me to shame. And Lynn puts us all to shame.*

The hardest part of prison for me is always seeing what is happening to those around me. I know my pain. I can talk and write around it but someone else's pain is the nightmare I can't describe. I'm going to do Gongyo now and chant for Lynn.

**April 24<sup>th</sup> Life Stories Group** Rose opened up about the things she'd seen and experienced as a black child in the deep south of America. It provoked much discussion. The strange white woman, who had dragged me around looking for the matches, has joined the group. She said, 'I'm not a racist but (the beginning of a statement which always confirms the views of the speaker) once in IT, a black woman shouted at me because I had a monkey on my screen.' Of course Sheila, even though she's white, had to have suffered racism.

'Someone called me a white wog when I was a kid.'

It is important to Sheila that she has suffered more than others, so we let her. She spoke of 'trying to dig the filth' out of her bones and she wears long sleeves in all weathers.

Rose said very little after Sheila spoke except to say, 'I was taught to hate white people by my mother. I hope God forgave her before she died.'

I've promised Rose that I'll go to her trial if I'm out of prison. She just wants to go home to America and she believes that her God will make this happen.


**April 24<sup>th</sup>** A dilemma today. I am teaching Iris' class but I also have a movement slip to go to the Job Centre. Yes there really is a place called the Job Centre in here. The appointment is so that the prison can call to get my state pension reinstated when I'm released.

181

Now this appointment was supposed to be for April 16th, the day before my expected release. I stood by the desk while the Job Centre woman told the clerk (a prisoner) to put this appointment on the computer. I watched the clerk do this. I saw her hand move the mouse and her index finger click its head. I saw it. But one week after my planned release I get the appointment. Now the dilemma. Today am I a teacher or a prisoner? Is my loyalty to my 'job' and 'students' stronger than my loyalty to my own wellbeing and if so, I really am a teacher. What to do? This 'foot in two camps' world is getting interesting. Should the prison be using an inmate as a teacher, giving me so much responsibility while having no control or power, no chance to make a decision about what the students really need to know and learn? I suppose this isn't much different from the outside world of teaching really.

**April 25th** 'I'm gonna kick off,' is a mantra used as a threat by a prisoner when she thinks she's not going to get something she wants or needs. It tells me that despite appearances to the contrary, we do have self-control, otherwise why don't we just 'kick off' anyway?

This morning one of the hard women, who has been working in the grounds, has been sacked from her job. She found this out from a slip of paper pushed under her door just before unlock. And for once I have a slither of sympathy for her. No notice, no warning, no reason – just sacked. To be sacked in prison means no money for tobacco, toothpaste, stamps or phone calls. I think she's going to 'kick off'.

**Lynn** Yesterday Lynn was asking to be moved.

'I can't take it in here,' she said.

The officer placated her with a promise to put in an app.

'I need help to do it,' Lynn said.

'I'll help you do it,' he promised.

As I was leaving for work this morning I asked the officer to send Lynn my way if she needed help to fill out anything. He looked at me strangely but said he'd do so. This woman haunts me.

The reply to my app came last night: *'Your ECL date is 14/05/09. If you are eligible you will be seen by the ECL clerk nearer the time.'*

Just to know that there is a list somewhere in this prison that has the names of the 18 day women, and to know that my name is on it, cheers me. Sometimes it feels as though I'm shouting into space. What is that line from 'Alien'? *'In space no one can hear you scream.'*

**April 25<sup>th</sup> After my visit** On the phone today Robbie told me that the police have been to our boatyard every day this week. It must be about Hess because little else would get them out. A vandalised car or a b u r g l e d  shed gets us only a crime

183

number, for insurance purposes. What it doesn't get us is a visit from a real live police officer. I wonder if someone with power, someone somewhere, will be able to call a halt to this or do powerful people come to the rescue only in works of fiction?

## DRESS CODE

I have noticed that some women walk around with one trouser leg rolled up, like a secret sign for members of a secret club. Perhaps it's a gang thing. Duffy does this but she's so friendly, even with her shaven head and name tattooed across the back of her neck. I couldn't imagine her in a gang. She was the first person to say hello to me on this wing. And I was so relieved, firstly because someone was friendly and secondly because it was Duffy. I want to ask her why she rolls up her trouser leg but I don't want to break an unwritten rule

**April 25<sup>th</sup> Dinner time** I had to come to prison to learn what a ciabatta is; it's a bread roll and I can't eat it. Tonight, when I reached the servery, all the salad had gone. Clare gave me the rest of hers. The kindness of the women in this place is always as startling to me as their rage. Tomorrow I'll give Clare my coffee and sugar.

**April 25<sup>th·</sup> 11:10 pm** Yesterday, during our phone call, my sister Jean mentioned the town where

I have placed Hess and today, during our visit, Robbie said that because of this Hess has to be moved. We can't take any chances that he is returned to Veronica. Locked in my cell, unable to speak to anyone, my mind is building scenarios of the police knocking on doors, taking Hess back. I can't stop thinking about it. I need to keep him safe. It would be even worse for him now because he has had two years of love and care. All I want is for the night to pass so that I can phone Robbie and hear his voice, reassuring and strong.

**April 26<sup>th</sup> Lunchtime** I'm watching the marathon on TV. I can see the Embankment and the river leading out of London and eventually to the sea. The sea is happiness to me, just as it was to my dad. The sea is life itself.

The dark night left me wanting to leave Washford and Somerset. It feels as though the entire county is corrupt, no honest people in power, no police officer who isn't caught up in this Alice in Wonderland story. When will someone begin to ask questions? Why would I rather go to prison than return Hess? When will someone ask that question?

**April 26<sup>th</sup> Afternoon** I've never wondered what the worst pair of trousers in the world would look like but if I had, I would now be able to describe them. They are tight, stretched lime green, narrow at the

185

ankle with a black line running down the seam and across the calf. They would be wrapped around a large woman who would be trying to dance aerobically outside my cell window, to a tuneless sound with a strong but soulless rhythm. It is Sunday afternoon and twenty women, led by a masculine female officer in trainers, have decided that they need to keep fit. Some are even smiling. God save us from pointless exercise.

I have turned over the page in my diary; I am looking at all of this week and next week then I can turn again, to freedom week. I have no idea where I am or what the outside of the prison looks like. Is there a car park? Shops? I arrived in the dark, through the small, blackened windows of the prison lorry. I arrived in the dark and in shock.

**April 27**th The weight is sliding from me and I'm getting worried. I eat everything I'm given and everything that is donated by other women but I just seem to be getting thinner. I arrived eight weeks ago today. Christine has been released, twenty days before the end of her sentence, not eighteen. The prison is so overcrowded that it's one out and one in, each cell never empty for more than a few minutes. The time has slowed for me now. I dream of sitting with Robbie, with friends, family, drinking tea and listening to people speaking in quiet voices.

186

**April 28th Before unlock** My back has gone again. I think it's the bed, a 2 inch thick foam mattress on a solid sheet of steel which is concreted into the wall, so there are no legs. I feel as though someone has turned a key in my spine and locked it. Just sitting, walking or lying down is painful. It's getting more difficult to walk and I have to grab my trousers to pull up my leg, just to take a step or climb the stairs.

Iris will, from today, be working next door in the beginners' class and Joe and I will be taking Iris' class. We shared the class yesterday and Joe, just like me, has no idea why Iris feels the need to push these women so much, to rush them through English. Iris, Joe told me, is worried what Pamela, their boss, will say. I didn't realise that Pamela was in charge. Iris thinks Pamela will be checking up on her and possibly find her lacking.

Iris' doctor parents retired to the Lake District. Her brother is also a doctor. It's my own background that colours and shapes my views. Isn't Iris' background 'secure', professional, middle class? What has happened to her to make her so hard, so insecure that she will bully foreign women, who are in prison, women with no power, no security, no money and no country? Will I never learn this lesson? Inside the perfect lives, the nightmares are hidden, just like any other. Are most people, as Thoreau believed, 'leading lives of quiet desperation'?

187

## BAD MANNERS

I had a 9 am appointment for a blood test, my third attempt, as on the two previous occasions I wasn't told that I had to fast. The nurse told me that I'd get another appointment this week so each night I have fasted, just in case. I went to class to let Joe know that I had an appointment and he let me go early. When I arrived, Manveer, an officer working in Health C a r e t h a t d a y , told me to go back to Education as my appointment wasn't for another ten minutes. I've noticed that some officers are on automatic rude, the one thing guaranteed to make me angry.

'OK, I'll go and sign back into Education, then turn around, sign out again and come back. That should take ten minutes. I have plenty of time,' I told him.

When I arrived back at Healthcare, the methadone sisters had filled the room. Manveer saw me standing at the gates but refused to acknowledge me or let me in. I waited in silence, finally turning my back on him and leaning against the gates. When another officer came along, I showed him my appointment slip and he let me in. Manveer wouldn't look at my slip to verify my appointment.

'Sit down!' he said.

'OK,' I said, forcing my mouth into a smile. I'm going to give you nothing you arrogant little bastard. He seemed a little peeved when, thirty seconds later, a nurse came out, spoke politely to me and took me in for my blood test. So back to

Education, with no food until lunchtime, because in prison we eat three times a day and there are no circumstances under which this routine can be changed. My back hurt so much that it was affecting my legs and once or twice they gave way. I felt ill.

At break Oana asked me to help her find a poem to send to her husband; next week is their 8th wedding anniversary. Joe gave us a movement slip and we went into the library.

'You can't come in here; we're doing induction!' shouted the library woman in the grey skirt with matching hair. I hate exclamation marks but Grey Woman spoke in exclamation marks so I have used them.

'Oh sorry, is there a notice on the door? I didn't see it,' I said, with raised eyebrows and much exaggerated politeness.

'No! Your teacher should have told you!'

'Our teacher sent us in here,' I replied, recognising the cul-de-sac I was travelling down but hoping that this time it may lead somewhere.

It is odd. Sometimes I am the teacher, being asked permission to go to the toilet, being shown movement slips. It is a schizophrenic experience.

We went back in the afternoon and exclamation mark woman had been replaced by a much more reasonable form of punctuation. Oana and I couldn't find a suitable poem so I wrote one for her, extracting pieces of information from her in order to build a picture.

'He's kind,' she told me, about the nameless, faceless man I was about to immortalise in hollow verse.

'Well tell me how he shows his kindness.'

'He's a good father.'

'Tell me what he does that makes him a good father.'

Oana ended up with a poem to which she signed her own name and in the afternoon we were allowed to go to the IT suite to type it.


## SING SONG

When I returned to the classroom this afternoon Joe was organising some language games for the foreign national women. We decided that it may be a good idea to teach them a traditional English song. Joe couldn't quite remember all of the words, given that the song was probably written when I was just a thirty second thought in my great granddad's head. But between us we had most of it. Mai, the livewire and back fixer, stood at the front of the whiteboard with a long ruler pointing to each word, while Joe and I went over it again and again, explaining that words have syllables and each syllable in this song has a note attached to it.

Finally we had something that resembled our song and so twenty women from as many countries, one prisoner, masquerading as a teacher and one teacher, born in the eighties with his heart in the sixties, sang 'Oh I Do Like To Be Beside the Seaside'.

The delight, the confused smiles and endearing accents made me, for that one moment, not want to be anywhere else but in that classroom, in that prison with those people.

**April 29**[th] Oana is angry and arrogant. She hates England and wants to go home to her husband and children in Romania. She speaks of England and the English as though Bronzefield is representative. She criticises the officers, saying they're stupid and unintelligent. Her eyes shine with rage. She cries for her children, complains constantly and boasts about her intellect. Indignant is Oana, and also a drug smuggler, having been arrested at the airport carrying 7kg of cannabis. I range from feeling insulted by her to feeling sad; today the former was winning.

Either Oana's arrogance has become more extreme or my patience more threadbare. This morning one of the other Romanian women shouted at her in their language. She too has children she misses. I don't know exactly what she said but I believe it was along the lines of, 'Stop whinging. We all miss our kids. Now just get on with it!' At least, that's what I hope she said.

### THE LOVELY DIANA

*Diana met her father for the first time when she was twelve. He began to buy her things; the high heels her mum wouldn't allow her to wear, the cigarettes,*

191

make-up. He allowed her to bunk off school. Her hero had arrived.

'I had a dad,' Diana said, 'for the first time.'

She wanted to be with him so she put herself in care then she ran away with him to Scotland, his home.

When she was thirteen Diana's dad put his penis in her mouth at knifepoint.

'He knew what he was doing. He never came inside me because he knew it would show. He never raped me because he knew they'd be able to tell. I was a virgin.'

Diana's mother came to Scotland and brought her back home. She told no one what her dad had done but he believed she was going to tell, so he obtained a two week prescription for methadone and sleeping pills went to Shaftesbury Avenue and committed suicide.

At fourteen Diana began smoking crack cocaine.
At fifteen she became a prostitute and heroin addict.

'Do you think what your dad caused you t o b e c o m e a heroin a d d i c t ?' I a s k e d her, h a l f expecting her to place the responsibility for her addiction on him.

'I don't know,' she said. 'Maybe I was just used to seeing it. My mum did it.'

One of the other women has told Diana that she has to forgive her dad before she can 'move on', that truly pointless and meaningless phrase. But at least she didn't use the word 'closure'. Why do we insist on trying to put a full-stop at the end of a part of our lives, *when that part will only ever warrant a semi-colon? Why do we accept these barren, lazy concepts from across the Atlantic? They gave us Otis Redding for god's sake. They gave us William Faulkner: I know they can do better than this.*

'I don't think you have to forgive him Diana; just don't give him any more of your life,' I told her, hoping that I wasn't falling into the same trap; looking for a simple solution. There is no solution to betrayal.

'I won't,' she said. 'I've won. He's dead and I'm alive so I've won. But I just want to know why he did it. He was a really clever man. He planned it. He knew exactly what he was doing. But I can't ask because he's dead. Last night I dreamed that he was standing behind me and I wanted to stab him. I want to know. And I want to stab him. I think about it now because the heroin's wearing off.'

I told Diana about the line from T.S. Eliot's 'The Wasteland'. 'April is the cruellest month,' he wrote.

'It's the cruellest month Diana because everything is coming alive after being frozen throughout the winter. When things thaw, when we thaw, we feel pain.'

## LOVE POEMS

I spent this afternoon, at the request of Beth, in the library sourcing love poetry to include in an anthology of poetry written by the women of

Bronzefield. I worked with Shirley, a young, gentle, shy black woman.

'I don't know much about poetry,' she said, slightly embarrassed. So we looked through books together. And that is how I found myself, on a sunny April afternoon, in a high security women's prison, reading aloud Sonnet 18 by William Shakespeare:

*'Shall I compare thee to a summer's day?*
*Thou art more lovely and more temperate:*
*Rough winds do shake the darling buds of May,*
*And summer's lease hath all too short a date:*
*Sometime too hot the eye of heaven shines,*
*And often is his gold complexion dimm'd;*
*And every fair from fair some time declines,*
*By chance, or nature's changing course, untrimm'd;*
*But thy eternal summer shall not fade*
*Nor lose possession of that fair thou ow'st;*
*Nor shall Death brag thou wand'rest in his shade,*
*When in eternal lines to time thou grow'st:*
*So long as men can breathe or eyes can see,*
*So long lives this, and this gives life to thee.*

Shirley didn't say anything. She sat with the mention of a smile on her face.

'I'm not s u r e  w h a t  it  m e a n s,' S h i r l e y s a i d  quietly, looking down at the grey formica desk.

'He's saying, just how lovely are you Shirley, as lovely as a summer's day? Nah. . . you're much hotter than that.'

**April 30<sup>th</sup>** When Becky is on duty we get last night's post and paper the next day. This morning, mixed in with my post, was the wing canteen list, the document that we all sign in order to receive our canteen items. Without it the officers can't give anything out, a consequence that would lead to screaming, shouting, swearing, threats and possibly violence.

I said 'Excuse me,' three times before the large, handsome, African officer stopped panicking long enough to see me holding out the list. His bright and relieved smile lit up the small side room where the canteen is given out. I received mine first.

### LIFE STORIES WITH BETH

The stories have the same bones to hold them up – rape, murder, incest, drugs, neglect, then the individual features of each story are added – a father here, an uncle there, each person giving the story a uniqueness in the familiarity of every cruel twist and turn. Snakes and Ladders of life. Some women climb a ladder, a few steps – another detox, another man, then another fix, another fist and down a snake to the pit again.

I've just received a card from Alice. She promised that she would write to me and I knew she intended to keep her word; I just wasn't certain if her life would get in the way of that. She's still clean and battling to stay that way. She says her friends are finding it hard that she isn't using any more and they seem to resent it.

I remember when our friend Jimmy stopped drinking and began going to the gym. One day he was in the pub and it was his friend Peter's turn to buy a round. Jimmy asked him for an orange juice and Peter put vodka in it.

Perhaps it's the courage of people like Alice and Jimmy that we find so hard to look at. Their courage highlights our cowardice, our excuses.

I've written back to Alice because she needs to know that I meant everything I said. I'm so proud of her. She inspires me.

**May 1st After breakfast** We have been given our medication and are now locked in our cells. 'Staff meeting,' we were told.

Yesterday in my post I received a copy of an interview given to the SGI Quarterly by Mariane Pearl, an SGI Buddhist and wife of Daniel Pearl, the journalist who was kidnapped and murdered in Pakistan. I believe some people are born to learn the lesson, the only lesson we have to learn, that clean and simple lesson of Shakyamuni's: everything comes down to our behaviour as a human being. Mariane Pearl has learned this lesson and now she is trying to teach us.

**8:45 am** Still locked in. No breakfast. The shouting and door kicking has begun.

**8:50 am** Unlocked, get breakfast. Reached servery at 9:00.

**9:05 am** Called to go to work so the choice is no breakfast and go to work or eat breakfast and get a warning for being late for work. I go to work.

### SOPHIE

[1]*Sophie is Italian. She is quietly spoken, shy and goes pink when she speaks. I immediately liked her.*

*Sophie's husband is an international lorry driver who asked her if she wanted to go with him on a delivery to England. Sophie didn't know that the lorry was carrying more alcohol than was stated on the paperwork. This was a way of avoiding paying so much excise duty. She and her husband were arrested in Kent and sent to prison. Her husband has pleaded guilty and is on his way home to Italy.*

*Sophie wishes to plead not guilty as she doesn't understand why an innocent person would plead otherwise. Her solicitor explained that if she pleads guilty she will, like her husband, be released and returned to Italy. If she pleads not guilty, as he advised, she will return to prison where she will wait, for an indeterminate length of time, until her trial at crown court comes up, where she may be found guilty and be returned to prison. Sophie is pleading guilty.*

**May 1st Afternoon** It's a four day holiday and I have set time aside to help Kate with her life story. I told her that I would correct her spelling and punctuation but would not alter anything else because it's her story, in her voice and no one can tell it except her.

Beth has asked if I will write two pieces, one for Black History Month, from the point of view of a white woman with a black child. The other piece is for an anthology of work on drug and alcohol abuse. I thought I may be able to tell some of John's story but I can only tell it from the outside. Little John's story is his to tell, not mine.

**Dinner time** This morning I saved my cornflakes for tonight because Friday, Saturday and Sunday is a small dinner, early lock up and I get very hungry. I've just discovered that my cornflakes have been taken. This morning someone asked me if I'd had breakfast because we didn't have time to eat. I told them that I save my cereal for the night because I get hungry. I can't remember who I spoke to but either she or another person knew the cornflakes were in my cell. Now, each day, I'll go to work knowing someone will be going into my cell looking for my carefully hidden food. It's going to be a long and hungry night. If I must look for something positive in this, as much as I don't want to, it is that my Omomori Gohonzon may have also been taken if it hadn't been kept from me. I could tell Diana or Duffy

198

or any of my friends in here but I know what will happen. They'll shout and swear on my behalf, draw attention to me, something I avoid at all costs in here.

The officer on duty is Manveer and he's angry with me because I didn't hear him calling my name. I was in my cell with the door closed, as always. This meant he had to walk up a flight of steps with my post and paper.

## YVONNE

*Yvonne is up for several crimes but the one crime she believed would put her in prison for five or six years is GBH. This week she went to court in front of a judge who is known to be harsh. He gave her six months. Without knowing the details and therefore having no images in my mind of beaten faces and broken bones, I gave her a celebratory hug in the corridor of the Education block where we meet each weekday.*

How prison gives us a comradeship, twists and moulds our beliefs and judgements, when we've come to know each other in this strange place, in fleeting conversations and shared hurts. I've watched Yvonne soften over the weeks, allowing her love for her man and her insecurity over him, to weep out.

**May 2$^{nd}$ After breakfast** I can hide my cornflakes or leave them in view with my note for the thief which says:

199

**'These cornflakes have been opened because I have spat in them so if you want to steal them, help yourself.'**

I've just finished reading some of Kate's life story. I particularly like that she doesn't write as a victim, trying to elicit a particular response. She isn't trying to tell me how to feel.

### KATE

*Kate has a broken nose; it's slightly sideways. She is small, blond and pretty, with an accent that slips and slides across Britain. What has saved her is that she was never sexually abused as a child so she still has a smile in her eyes. Her nose was broken at age thirteen by a punch in the face from a Scottish policeman. He'd caught her stealing and handcuffed her to a railing. But because her wrists were so small she was able to slip her hand out and she made a run for it. She was caught and punched. Her broken nose and blackened eyes were never investigated; after all, Kate was a thief.*

**3:00 pm** The shouting and screaming and general tantrums are now just boring, disturbing as they do the quiet of my cell. Have a tantrum if you like, but please do it quietly.

**3:50 pm** As there appears to be no correlation between the volume of the shouting, the frequency of the swear words and the speed at which the person shouting gets what they want, I can only assume that this method worked for them as children until their emotional age was stopped and frozen in ice by their father's penis.

**May 3$^{rd}$ After breakfast** No one is really going anywhere until the end of our sentence. Despite this fact there are a percentage of women, 30% to be pedantic, who have to jump the queue. . . any queue. We may be queuing for someone to shit in our mouth but these women will still try to get there first.

**The Visit** Ayesha, a young, pale-skinned, mixed-race girl was next to me in the prison queue. She's only been in prison a few days.

'Who's come to see me?' she asked the officer.

'Delia,' the officer replied.

'Oh no, not my sister.'

'Are you going to get nagged?' I asked her.

'Yes. She's got a good job. Doesn't smoke, doesn't drink. She's a good girl.'

'And you're the interesting one,' I said.

Ayesha looked startled and then smiled a glorious smile.

'No one's ever called me that before but yeah ...I'm the interesting one.'

On the way out I asked her how her visit had been.

'Did you get nagged?'

201

'No. She just cried a lot. She's very emotional my sister. She's very feminine. But she's OK. I'm glad she's like that.'

Back in the block Lizzie warned me that the two new girls are thieves.

'Thanks,' I say.

'One has just nicked someone's make-up and is blaming the other,' Lizzie said and I wonder if one of them had taken my cornflakes.

## KARLY

*Karly is worried. Her fifteen year old brother has the mental age of a nine year old and three weeks ago his mum sent him off to Africa with a man she'd known for just a few days. Their return is overdue by two weeks.*

'*What would you do Lin?*'

'*What would I do? I'd get in touch with Social Services as soon as possible that's what I'd do.*'

*Karly said she'd spoken to an officer about it but she doesn't know if he's going to do anything. Karly can't phone Social Services because she doesn't have the number and even if she did, if it's not on her list of approved numbers, she can't phone them.*

'*Go and speak to him again. Keep on!*' *I told her.*

**May 4**[th] Time has slowed and ten days feels as though I'm walking towards the horizon. I felt exhausted today because I'm not sleeping.

I did some more proofreading for Kate and learned that she has been in prison thirty times. She's thirty-five. Kate was involved in the fight with the officers a couple of weeks ago.

'They screwed with my meds and I was off my head. I don't remember anything,' she told me.

She attacked Colin, a senior officer.

'I kicked him in the balls and was put in isolation.'

When I told her I wasn't sleeping she offered me her Valium, which I declined.

'I'm sorry. I don't mean for you to get a habit,' Kate said.

She explained that often women who don't use, end up with a drug habit when they come to prison. I told her that I usually use Rescue Remedy but they took it off me when I arrived. Kate said that they also gave her 'Kalms' which she offered to me.

Just before dinner she went off to get her meds and then gave me her 'Kalms' in a small piece of tissue as she passed me on the stairs. I took them immediately and they've definitely taken the edge off. I feel quite floaty in fact, the result of a clean system I suppose.

Another bully has arrived in 2A. She makes a point of going straight to the front of the queue, not sneakily like some, but brazenly in front of the officers, as if to say, 'Stop me!' They don't. Weak or disinterested officers make a dangerous place lethal. I'm going to phone Bullyline to get it stopped. I'm out next week but there are a couple of quiet women in here and some pregnant ones. We're supposed to rely on the officers to sort out this type of thing and not try to sort it out ourselves. Say anything to this woman and it'll end up on the floor. Then a warning will be issued to both parties, because weak officers react, not respond, and a warning may interfere with my release. This would never have happened on Beverley's watch.

**May 5**th Today there was no cereal at the servery so I had a choice: continue avoiding bread to try to sort out my bleeding bowels and go hungry, or eat the toast. Being weak willed I chose to eat the bread. When I got into line Lizzie was having a heated argument with Bully Girl about the volume of her music last night.

'She thinks she's a "rude girl" but she's just disrespectful,' Lizzie said.

'I blame the officers. They watch her walk to the front of the line and do nothing about it so she thinks she can do what she likes.'

This was my way of letting off steam while standing safely behind Lizzie's spirit. Lizzie's roommate was also angry and asked me if I'd heard Bully Girl's music.

'Yes, I heard it. It was blaring!'

I hadn't actually heard it as the Kalms gave me a good night's sleep, but I could filter my anger at her queue jumping through these two plucky women and still stay reasonably safe. I'm really surprised that Bully Girl is acting up, as she doesn't have the six friends with her that she usually needs in order to surround a pensioner and steal her purse.

**May 6<sup>th</sup> Before breakfast** Yesterday Oana asked me to write another poem for her, this time it was to send to her best friend in Romania. Pamela gave us a movement slip for thirty minutes and we went to work in the library. A handful of women were being loud with that invitation on their faces that said, 'Go on. Stop us.'

I wrote the poem. I know Oana is passing these poems off as her work, just as she did the one I wrote for her husband. I don't care. If I can't put this ego aside for a handful of poems given to a young, drug smuggling Romanian woman, what does this say about me? Besides, they're not very good, difficult as it is to write deeply felt emotions about someone I have never met. It must be a bit like the Poet Laureate being asked to write a poem about a Royal she has neither met nor admired.

Oana's best friend is looking after things at home while she is in prison and I'll give Oana her due, I've seen a photo of this woman and she is gorgeous. Don't think I'd leave someone who looks like that around Robbie. Don't think I'd leave most women around Robbie. That makes Oana a far bigger person than me.

The officer left my door flap open last night and now I need a poo but don't want to be caught on the loo, or worse still, wiping my bottom during unlock. Oh to have a leisurely, private poo. Not long now.

I could hear the keys j a n g l i n g along the hall and it sounded as though they'd reached my door. Then someone distracted the officer a n d I can hear people getting their breakfast but I'm still locked in. Just as Poe was able to capture everyone's greatest terror in 'Premature Burial', tucked into a crevice in my mind, along with the abduction and torture of one of my grandchildren, is a picture of a forgotten me, locked in my cell forever, screams unheard, a space in the queue unnoticed.

**After breakfast** Lizzie has told me that we're locked up all morning for staff training.

Kate came into my cell again last night and gave me her Kalms. I gave her some sugar.

'Is there anything that would stop y o u coming to prison again?' I plucked up the courage to ask.

'Yeah . . . not getting caught.'

I persevered.

'If you went into a shop with £1000 in your bag, would you steal?'

'Yes. I can't stop. I give it all away. My Steve has money. He tells me he'll buy me anything I want. But I can't stop. It's an addiction.'

Kate knows Ellie. Ellie wrote down her address for me before she was released but I lost it between cell moves.

'Can you get a message to Ellie for me? I don't want her to think it was just talk. I want her to know that she can call me if she needs anything. She was good to me when I was in here. She's a lovely girl with a big heart.'

'No one has seen Ellie since she got out but that's a good thing. She's not in the area shoplifting. Maybe she's trying to sort herself out,' Kate said.

'She told me that she wanted to change her life. I taught her to chant. I gave her my number and Robbie's number. But she thinks I was coming out in April. I don't want her to think I didn't mean it.'

Kate said that she'd get her Steve to pass a message on to Ellie's mum, a woman who, according to Ellie's description, seems to be picking up the pieces of many lives and gluing them into a family.

**May 7th 2:15 pm** They've decided not to let us out of our cells – no reason, no warning, no explanation, just locked in here and no idea how long for.

A young, quietly spoken and painfully beautiful Iranian woman, an over-stayer, two months pregnant, arrived in the ESOL class last week, accompanied by another young Iranian. Yesterday she showed me her paperwork, hoping that I could explain the 18 day early release and HDC quagmire. She is here until July if she gets her HDC, otherwise it's September. Today she asked me how she might be moved to a quieter place in the prison.

'There is no quiet place in prison,' I told her. Then I said, 'Get an app and I'll help you fill it out.'

A long explanation with hand signals followed. She wishes to share with the other Iranian woman so that they may have someone to talk to in a language they understand.

At one point I had four people, all from different parts of the world, asking me questions on prison, immigration, deportation, questions to which I have no answers. I was at screaming pitch, as these four were surrounded by ten other women, speaking in several languages. I believe the noise would finish me off if I was here for much longer. The young Iranian woman seemed unconvinced that I could do nothing for her except help with the app. What puzzles me is the amount of stress she appears to be suffering and from a woman in whose country adulterous women are buried up to their necks in dirt and stoned to death.

### THE CASE OF THE UTENSILS CASE

**May 8**<sup>th</sup> On the wall behind the servery is a glass-fronted case which measures approximately 3ft by 3ft and is approximately eight inches deep. It is kept locked until the servery is unlocked, then the officer unlocks this case also. There is a special key on his substantial set of keys just for this case. In the case and on display is an array of kitchen utensils: spatulas, whisks, serving spoons. When I first saw the case, and the security surrounding it, I got the serious giggles, which I had to swallow in case one of the other women thought I was laughing at her. I began to wonder how long it would be before the government decided to wage war on crimes involving stainless steel utensils. I could even write their slogan; 'Use a whisk; go to jail!'

## SPINDLES FARM

Spindles Farm is on the news. Father, mother, son and both daughters have been found guilty of animal cruelty and will be sentenced next month. One of them may even see the inside of a prison, where they will be forced to eat dinner sitting next to the non-payers of council tax and the foreign student over-stayers.

I knew it wasn't a good idea to watch the report; a warning was given but I have a compulsion to watch these things. I have now fallen down a dark well and even thoughts of going home next week can't lift me out. My questions are always the same: How many people phoned the RSPCA? How many calls did it take before they went out? How does it feel for an animal to be lying down, dying of disease, hunger and thirst, watching those who can help just walk by? What does it feel like to feel nothing?

**May 8th After lock up** For the first time since being in prison I returned to the servery after dinner and asked for extras for the long night ahead. I was given two packets of crisps and a flapjack. The anticipation of eating these makes me look forward to the night.

Because Bronzefield refuses to confirm either a visit or a release date until the very last minute, it is impossible to look forward to either. A lost scrap of paper, a clerk with a cold or a wayward husband, a missed word, an unticked box, these things can keep us here. So yes, I am probably going home on Thursday May 14th and no, I can't think about this with any sense of excitement. Giving my old mum a cuddle, playing with my grandchildren, drinking tea with friends, making love with Robbie, all of these are withheld, locked in a case where I can see them but can't have them, just like the spatulas.

My 10:30 visit in the morning has not been confirmed by a visit slip pushed under my door, although my prison account slip and a card from a well-wisher have. Both were delivered separately. Do they walk back and forth across the yard carrying each separate piece of paper or do they simply and deliberately hold on to the most important piece until the very last minute? So the night ahead will be one of tears and ripped nails. I can't say if any of this is deliberate or simply the result of incompetence and it doesn't really matter. The result is the same. And for this reason I don't mind when a woman kicks and screams and bangs her door. I just try to imagine what kind of emotional torment has been inflicted on her in order to elicit that response.

**9:00 pm** I'm listening for footsteps, gates being locked and unlocked, keys rattling on the chain of an officer who is carrying my visiting slip, ready to push it under my door. But it doesn't come. My head hurts.

**10:35 pm** Next week's Visiting Order has been pushed under my door but nothing for the morning's visit. What is happening?

**10:50 pm** It's here! No footsteps, no keys rattling, just a silent glide under the door.

**11:15 pm** In each cell there is an intercom button to be used in order to contact an officer. I've never used it and never will, not out of self-control or stubbornness. I won't use it out of fear, the fear that no one will respond, that there's nothing at the other end except a screaming silence.

**May 9th.** Tomorrow I can turn the page in my 'Day One Christian Ministries' Diary and then I'll be on the week that I'm supposed to be going home. If I stay up late tonight, at midnight I can turn it over and look at May 14$^{th.}$

My blood tests have been returned with an apparent problem and an appointment with the doctor on Monday; no nurse, go straight to jail and the doc. Of course I'm already planning my funeral: wicker coffin, so I can break out if I'm not really dead. Everyone crying. Please don't come to 'celebrate' my life. Why should they be having a good time if I can't join in? I want wailing. Tell lies about me. Make things up. I don't care as long as the lies make me seem like a better person. Isn't that what we do at funerals; make the person into someone we wish they'd been?

## MIND GAMES

On April 30$^{th}$ I sent in an app asking for my book, 'The Grass Arena', a book Chris had posted to me on April 20$^{th}$ but hadn't arrived. On May 5$^{th}$ my app, clearly dated April 30$^{th}$, was returned to me stating that I had received the book on April 28$^{th}$, two days before I sent in the app asking for it. On May 6$^{th}$ the book arrived in my cell.

**May 9$^{th}$ 4:00 pm** The visit was wonderful but I can't tell myself it is the last one as I don't know. I just can't risk the hope.

## SPINDLES FARM

There is a report on Spindle Farm in the Independent today, followed by an appeal by the RSPCA for funds to help the rescued horses. The appeal took up almost as much room as the report. I have written a letter to the Independent:

*'I would like to congratulate the RSPCA on their operation at Spindle Farm last y e a r  w h i c h  l e d to the successful prosecution of five members of the Gray family and the rescue of many horses and ponies. I would also like to ask the RSPCA if they would consider responding to the following questions:*

*On which date was the RSPCA first a l e r t e d that there was a possible case of cruelty and/or neglect at Spindle Farm?*

*How many phone calls did the RSPCA receive regarding Spindle Farm before they began their investigation?*

*How much time elapsed between the initial alert and the initial attendance by an RSPCA officer?*

*When James Gray was convicted in October 2006 of causing unnecessary suffering to a horse, did the court ban him from keeping horses for a period of time? If this was the case, what steps did the RSPCA and police take to ensure that this ban was being followed?*

*Yours faithfully*
*Lin Tidy (HMP Bronzefield)'*

I wonder if my letter will be published. I wonder if my letter will leave the prison.

**May 9th After lock up** Kate has been put on 'basic'. A new officer (sweeping clean!) has accused her of passing medication to her friend Ozzie. Being on 'basic' means less canteen money, lock up all day, except for meals, and no TV. Kate has rearranged her new TV-free cell.

'I've made room so I can do more writing. It's probably a good thing. I can crack on with my life story and do a bit more reading.'

Kate must be a bane to the prison. They just can't get to her. And her attitude is the antithesis of mine. I'd be moaning and full of resentment towards the officer and life in general.

I gave her today's Independent and magazine. She has 'The Buddha, Geoff and Me' and a copy of the interview with Mariane Pearl. I must get over myself, always thinking I have something to give someone. Who am I to say whose life is a success and whose is a failure?

I thought Kate was a bigamist but she's not; she's a trigamist. Is this a victimless crime? Is a crime still a crime if there's no victim?
Ponder, ponder.

**May 9th 10:45 pm** Rose is convinced that her Lord is going to get her out of crown court and

214

home to the USA, an innocent woman, so she's pleading not guilty. I am going to court, just as one friendly and familiar face in a foreign land. I have no idea if Rose is guilty or not. The charge is 'importation of drugs'. Part of the evidence against her is a text on her phone which she received when she landed. The text said, 'Are you safe?'

**May 10<sup>th</sup> Before breakfast** Oana went to court on Thursday, along with her brother-in-law, and pleaded guilty to importing 7kg of cannabis. She was expecting to receive eighteen months to two years. The judge gave them both a year, after hearing that they wanted to go home to Romania, never to return to the UK. So one year, halved, as is the system, minus some time off because they're being deported means Oana will be going home in a few days.

Question (with Sophie in mind). If someone pleads guilty in order to receive a lighter sentence, when they are in fact not guilty, are they committing perjury?

### LEVEL 4 HEALTHCARE

If a prisoner in Bronzefield is on medication they are not told when their prescription needs to be renewed. They find out when they reach the end of the queue for their meds. The nurse who gives out the meds is unable to renew their prescription so the process is: prisoner puts in an app to see the doctor to get her prescription renewed. Bronzefield has a

215

'nurse first' system so the prisoner has to see the nurse first. The nurse then refers the prisoner to the doctor. The prisoner waits for this appointment. By this time a week may have elapsed. So a prisoner on medication for epilepsy or diabetes or high blood pressure can go without it for up to a week. This is why Kate was fighting with the officers. Kate is on an anti-psychotic drug and her prescription ran out. She told me, 'Some women cut themselves badly so that they can see a doctor who will renew their prescription quickly.' Question: What is prison for?

**May 10<sup>th</sup> 11:00 are** Kate is locked up all day as this is part of the 'basic' punishment. I'm still proofreading her life story and her voice comes through so clearly. Kate has managed to write something that could so easily have ended up on the 'misery' shelf at WH Smiths but her sparky, smiley enthusiasm shines through.

The dying horses of Spindle Farm have formed an aching lump in my chest. How is it possible to walk past? To switch off is one thing; having nothing to switch off is another.

### ASSOCIATION TIME

In the block the women scream and shout and laugh, loud and empty, their eyes never catching the joke. The noise, the noise. Outside my window the women sit or lounge on the grass or walk around and around the triangle. But always, always, is the music pounding and endless.

I'm reading, 'The Color of Water' by James McBride, a book I borrowed from the prison library. I found it in the 'New Arrivals' box and my stamp is the first on the clean white ticket. This is a magical book written by someone with a beautiful soul.

Paula, my racist ex-neighbour, studiously ignores me when we see each other. I know she wasn't happy with me. I made her feel uncomfortable so I don't exist to her. Besides, she owes me a pen and she hasn't forgotten it.


**May 11<sup>th</sup> Breakfast and meds** In the meds queue this morning was a woman whose 18 day early release is also on Thursday. I heard her say, 'I wish they'd tell me if I'm going. They're messing people around. Some people are still here after their 18 days. '

My stomach is now knotted and I'm on the loo. I have finished Gongyo but my courage has left me. It is always a temptation to ask for a solution 'out there' at times of fear.

Today I have a doctor's appointment and I'll find out about my blood tests. I could ask Robbie to book me a doctor's appointment for Friday, just to get everything going, but of course I can't; I may still be here.

Received yesterday's paper today.

**May 11<sup>th</sup> After lunch lock up** We won't be told if we're going home on Thursday until Wednesday. Official. It may even be Wednesday night, allowing us no more anticipation and joy than is absolutely necessary.

Yesterday the young, beautiful and pregnant Iranian over-stayer told me that she had $350 Canadian dollars when she was arrested by the Heathrow Airport police. When she arrived at Bronzefield this had been converted to £130. I checked the exchange rate in the Independent and it was $1.91 to the pound and she is wondering where her $100 approximately has gone.

'I don't know,' I told her. 'This is England.'
Shrug.


**May 11<sup>th</sup> After dinner** A young woman had an epileptic seizure outside the library today. She was on the floor for about thirty minutes. It seemed to go on forever. I was sitting at the table, in front of the large window, having been given a movement slip. All the while she was down a young officer called Ivana knelt down beside her, holding a jumper under her head, gently touching her arm, trying to ensure she didn't harm herself, while the young woman span, her feet propelling her. I waited for the ambulance but none came.

Kate came to see me. She's been in many prisons, many times, including Holloway. She believes Bronzefield to be the worst.

'No one cares in here,' she said.

When Kate came to Bronzefield in February 2008 she had a breakdown and didn't leave her cell for six months, except to shower and eat. Not association, not work, not education, nothing. She never saw a doctor and was never medicated.

'I was like a zombie. I just sat in my cell. I couldn't speak. They just left me. It's a new, shiny place but it's all show. Underneath there's nothing.'

**May 12$^{th}$** My mind is outside of this prison. I didn't want it to be but I can't get May 14$^{th}$ out of my thoughts and that's why the noise is louder and the jabbering voices have multiplied. My outside life has crept into my cell; it's standing in the corner, hands on hips, sneering.

**May 12$^{th}$ In the classroom with J o e .** Joe has decided to teach the women an English joke and looks to me for support:

### THE DOG'S NOSE JOKE

**JOE**: An English joke OK? My dog's got no nose.

**BEATRICE**: Why no nose?

**JOE**: No! Joke! My dog's got no nose. How does it smell?

219

**BEATRICE**: You do this? You take dog's nose?

**JOE**: No Beatrice. The dog doesn't really have no n o s e.

**BEATRICE**: Why you say 'no nose'? I don't understand.

**JOE**: You see, I say, 'My dog's got no nose,' then you Say, 'How does it smell?' and I say, 'Awful!'


SILENCE..............


**SAHRA**: Some dog have flat nose. Why this?

Tomorrow, May 13th, is the end of Mai's sentence. She has been told that she won't be released. She doesn't know why and today I've watched her eyes slowly darken. In class she banged her small hand so hard on the desk that paper and people jumped. She is hardening and the smiles that were always there have gone.

The room spun a few times today as the questions on immigration, probation, court, HDC and ECL flew at me in a variety of accents. I completed three apps for people as best I could but for most questions I simply went on to refine my Bronzefield shrug.

## VALENTINA

***May 12<sup>th</sup> After dinner*** *There's a beautiful Russian woman called Valentina in 2A, tall with waist length hair the colour of horse chestnuts. She seems to be attaching herself to me; I think she's lonely and a bit scared. Valentina told me that she left prison on an 18 day early release and went to the address she had given probation. After a few days her landlord told her she had to leave as she was renting a council house from someone who was renting it from the council. She and her two children went to her mother's home. She forgot to tell probation so she is in breach of her licence and has been returned to prison.*

*Tonight she brought me an app on which she's asked for confirmation of her release date. Probation responded on May 1<sup>st</sup> with a provisional release date but is waiting to see if the court wishes to add another 44 days for breach of her licence. I wrote out her next app for her, advising her to wait until May 19<sup>th</sup>, giving probation 19 days to get the information from the court. She thanked me and gave me a hug. Valentina returned five minutes before lock up while I was doing evening Gongyo. She asked me what I was doing.*

'I'm a Buddhist. These are my evening prayers.'

'Buddhist? You have God?'

221

*'No, no God.'*

*'What you believe?'*

*I pointed to my heart. 'I believe we all have Buddhahood. A great thing.'*

*'Power?' she asked.*

*'Yes, power.'*

*'What else?'*

*'Cause and effect. A good thing out, a good thing in.*

*A bad thing out, a bad thing in.'*

*'You teach me?'*

*'Yes, tomorrow I teach you.'*

**May 12th 10:00 pm** It was reported in the Independent today that Kenneth Clarke, the Shadow Business Secretary, avoided the full rate of council tax on his two homes by claiming that neither of these is his main residence. He said that his main home was in his constituency, claiming a 2nd home allowance on his home in London. The tax payer then paid the council tax on this. Among the Bronzefield

222

population, (Category A) are several women who are serving prison sentences for non- payment of council tax. I feel a shrug coming on.

**May 13<sup>th</sup> Morning**   Gongyo before breakfast. Fear in my guts giving me a loose and fast morning poo. What is on the computer today? Am I going home tomorrow or did someone's biscuit break off in mid- dunk, resulting in them forgetting to press the mouse in the column marked 'release'?

The Campaign Against Prison Slavery (CAPS) is an organisation doing what it says. In Bronzefield some women work for £2 a day making things for Dr Barnardos. The profits from their crafts go to this charity. Some prisons involve private companies which sell the prisoner's products and keep the profits. CAPS is trying to stop this. Wouldn't it be a better idea to donate any money created to the victims of crime instead of towards a Managing Director's holiday in the Bahamas. Another rhetorical question and another absent question mark.

**May 13<sup>th</sup> 4:45 pm**   No news of my release. I had my pre-release medical this afternoon and the nurse began to panic about my blood results. They show a thyroid problem but of course I've had this for years. I forgot to tell them about it when I arrived. In my fear and shock the only thing I could remember was my bi-polar condition and my high blood pressure. I wonder if the prison sends for a prisoner's medical records. Clearly mine weren't sent for or perhaps they sit under a stack of missing Independents, for which Robbie has paid.

My head feels full of rocks and the tears are lurking. Good news or bad will make me cry. What a cruel system.

Oana was sentenced last week and was told today that she's going home to Romania tomorrow. Mai is being deported to Malaysia. Adriana is in court on May 27th.


**May 13th 7 pm** The release list hasn't arrived or been read and now I'm locked up for the night just not knowing. Manveer, the laziest, rudest and most ignorant officer I've met so far, told me, and the other May 14th woman, that he'd let us know tonight when the list arrived. He promised but I knew; something in his manner, empty, soulless, told me he wouldn't, not couldn't, but wouldn't. I want to smash my cell, tell them to shove their 18 days, at least then I'll know when I'll be going home, June 1st, before 9 am.

Robbie told me, 'It's a game. Don't let them win.'

If I withdraw my 18 day ECL then I've won. I came into prison a terrified woman, too terrified to be anything but polite and compliant. I leave an angry woman but not because I've been to prison; I committed a crime and prison is where criminals go. I'm angry because the system isn't satisfied with a prisoner simply doing their sentence, they have to be tormented as well, and I have no idea if this is deliberate or not. I also have no idea if this would make any difference. But at least if it was deliberate then there is a modicum of control over it somewhere out there. I could then fight it, be angry with it and decide to win the game.

**May 13<sup>th</sup> 9:00 pm** I've been trawling the Gosho for some guidance but all I feel is resentment, rage and helplessness. Kate told me tonight that I'd helped many people since I'd been in here but I can't seem to believe this or even care. I can't even seem to help myself. I can do the time. Just tell what that time is.

**May 13<sup>th</sup> 11:15 pm** Nichiren reminded me tonight that all I have to do is chant and do my best. This is all I need to do. I have to remember that I put me in here. I chose to take Hess and not return him. To accept this responsibility gives me control over my life. No one has done this to me, not Veronica, not Judge Simpton. I did this to myself. I chose to do this to myself. To understand this is to know that I am not in a cell, even when I am in one. Thank you Nichiren.

**May 14<sup>th</sup> 12:35 am** I have been sitting on the floor in the dark, c h a n t i n g. Against t h e w a l l are my clear plastic bags filled with my belongings, ready for my release. Whether it is t o d a y o r J u n e 1<sup>st</sup> I won't unpack these bags again. One carries only my cards and letters, numbering several hundred; this is the heaviest one of all. I can't sleep. My mind is a travelling circus. My poor Robbie had to listen to my whining on the phone and I feel ashamed. He told me that he's coming t o Bronzefield at 10 am to collect me and intends to 'kick up a stink'. If only he knew how p o i n t l e s s that would be. A machine has no reasoning, no logic, and no compassion. We're back where we started.

A realisation. I c o u l d have entered prison kicking and screaming, trashing my cell, attacking officers, refusing to work and it would have made no difference to anyone. Nothing touches, nothing reaches, nothing changes. The people who run this place would be on the floor in a heap if they'd had the lives of some of these women, women who are still standing and hoping, still singing, still giving their fruit to a pregnant stranger.


**May 14<sup>th</sup> 7:49 am** A few women noticed that I was sitting downstairs at the table waiting for the Freedom List. One or two came to speak to me, to reassure me that it would be OK. It was a lovely thing

226

to do. If I am still here tonight I will teach Valentina to chant.

The problem with all of this is that I've never been very good at mind games. I don't even realise that I'm involved in one until it's too late. Bronzefield is a mind game and I didn't realise. Would I have done anything differently had I known? Probably not. Because when hope is offered, it is human nature to cling o n t o it. So, when on March 5th I was told that I'd be going home on April 17th, I clung to that date and found myself drowning when it was too late. And when they threw me May 14th, I clung to that also.

**May 14th 8:35 am** After asking for a complaint form while I was on the phone to Robbie this morning, a prisoner told me that I'm going home today. She also told me to take all of my prison-issue clothes, cup, plate, flask and plastic cutlery with me to Reception otherwise I'd be sent back to get it. The officers failed to tell me this. I still don't want to hope or smile or laugh or look at the outside of this place. I can't afford to do this just yet. They may change their minds. It may be a computer error. Or a joke.

I've given Diana my toiletries; she asked me a week ago if she could have them. Kate has my stamps and envelopes a n d wanted nothing from me, even though I asked her.

227

I realise, perhaps too late, that I have been watched and protected from a distance by a few women in here. An occasional check, 'How you doing?' Someone coming into my cell to check that the woman who had just left my cell hadn't been asking me for anything. Care and concern from strangers simply because I was both one of them and yet, somehow, not one of them. My fear when I came in here was that I'd be seen as weak, a victim, someone to bully. Maybe I am all of these things but for some women this has brought out the need to protect me, perhaps because there was no one to protect them when they needed it.

**May 14th 9:09 am** Waiting to be called so I'll chant in Cell 26, Wing 2, Spur A, Bronzefield Prison, for the last time. I never had time to teach Valentina to chant. My cell is cleared, ready for the next woman. All that is left are the boxes of Tampax, which were here when I arrived, and the envelope still stuck to the wall with toothpaste; on it is written, 'Freedom Is a State of Mind'.

**May 14th 12:30 pm** I wandered out of the gates, not knowing where I was and then I heard 'Oi!' Robbie was walking towards me and we cuddled. I felt so safe.

He took my black, prison-issue holdall in which I'd managed to smuggle out my prison journal that was to become this book. I don't know what I was expecting; it is difficult to rush into someone's arms carrying a large holdall weighing at least 30lbs.

A young Oriental woman, with little English, and a rough as nuts English woman were released with me. We'd been held up for a couple of hours while the officers searched for the English woman's ID, which they finally found hidden in her vagina.

'It's the only ID I've got,' she complained. 'How am I gonna get any money without ID?'

The various rooms and hoops through which we had to walk each twisted my stomach; would this be the one that would stop me leaving? Would it be a still angry Judge Simpton, whose threats and confidence in his licence to do anything he wished, a clerical error, a tea stain on a calendar? Any of these could find me back in my cell. Not until I was sitting next to Robbie in his red, older than it looked, Iveco, would I believe that I could walk through a door without waiting for the slow steps of an officer to unlock it, that I could select my own food and speak with whoever I chose, when I chose and for as long as I chose.

I had asked Robbie to drop off the young Oriental woman at the train station. I said to her, 'Do you have money?'

'No, no money,' she said in her utilitarian English, believing that we were asking her to pay for the lift. Robbie gave her £20, which she tried to refuse, finally taking it when our insistence wore her down. We said goodbye and good luck. I gave her a quick hug, this woman with whom I had so much to share, about whom I knew so little.

Robbie asked me if I was hungry and I said I was because I wanted the experience of e a t i n g with him again. He took me to a motorway service station where I had a proper cup of tea and a prawn sandwich in crusty bread. I left my bowels to worry about themselves. The tea was the colour of Solomon in July and seemed even more so having spent the weeks drinking prison tea the colour of snails.

Then we went to Frome to see my mum. She was bent double in her armchair, where she'd spent the past two years, being hoisted out for a wash or to use the commode. She was staying alive to see my brother married. I knew that. I think we all knew that.


**May 23<sup>rd</sup> John and Barbara's wedding** Mum made it and so did I. It was worth the extra month in prison to see my brother finally marry the woman he'd loved for over forty years. I'd always felt that it was my job to protect him and now I could hand that job over to Barbara, a woman who wanted John's happiness more than she did her own. That is my definition of love and now my brother is loved.

By this time Robbie and I had also decided to marry and the date was set for January 23<sup>rd</sup> at Taplow Court, the SGI Buddhist Centre in Berkshire. Lists were made and money paid for the reception. Robbie was so excited. He told everyone he met and in turn everyone was happy for us and said so. The sun was shining on our heads too. After seventeen years we would officially tell the world that our love had survived and would continue.

During this time my ego was polished to a golden glow with yellow ribbons on my boat and the congratulations and praises of friends and neighbours. The phrase, 'stuck to your principles' was bounced around and I became weary of explaining that I hadn't gone to prison for a principle; I had gone to prison for a dog called Hess. I was being moulded into something I wasn't, a principled person. I was simply a woman whose skin was so thin, it absorbed too much pain.

## JUNE 2009

Detective Freeman, the same officer who had called Robbie when I was in prison, called him again. This time he asked him to go to Bridgewater Police Station. This was the shiny new station, replacing the one in Seaton which had begun to resemble the worst possible block of council flats, designed by an architect who clearly had issues with the poor. Robbie ignored the request, an action we would later regret when we came to realise that Detective Freeman was less than devoted to his given task and was somehow giving us a chance. What kind of chance we didn't know.

June was also a time of excitement, gigs, wedding plans, and a trip to Cornwall on the bike.

And a time to talk of things we'd talked of before, sound friendships and raw betrayals.

People had written statements for me, accompanied me to court, cared for Bob for the weeks in which I was in prison, as I worried that Robbie would be too busy to do a careful job of it, written to me, supported me and loved me. Not all of them agreed with my actions but all of them knew that these actions came from my heart and nowhere else.

The betrayals were painful, especially for Robbie. Ken, a long-time friend of both of us, gave a statement to the police and then appeared in the magistrates' court as a witness for the prosecution. At the same time as this he also approached Robbie in a local shop and, with tears in his eyes, said that he was sorry and had he known how Veronica was treating Hess he would never have given that statement. His evidence was based on his views of Veronica from his boat, walking Hess on the beach.

Ken had also been one of the first people to take up the offer to buy a mooring from the owners of the marina. The sale of these moorings was the beginning of the end of our unique community. Living on a boat equates with freedom. The knowledge that we can move our home to wherever there is water is the belief that boat livers cling to. The reality is somewhat different of course. Moorings for all but the smallest of vessels are scarce, so the abiding threat of eviction is the rolled up newspaper that controls us. But to buy a mooring is to give up on the dream, no matter how fanciful that dream may be and ironically, in that marina, it also gives no more protection against eviction. One man, who had bought one of these moorings, was given an eviction order when he used a boat insurance company that wasn't approved by the marina owners. He fought to stay on his mooring but had to spend thousands of pounds in barrister's fees in order to do so.

So Ken was scared. He was scared of the power he believed his landlords had to evict him and generally make his life uncomfortable. So he vocally opposed the setting up of a residents' association, even believing the owners' threat that, should one be formed, they would close the marina. It was so sad to watch such a hard-working man, a man who had protected his family for so long, buckle under the pressure put on him by such ruthless people. We had watched Ken and his wife Janet for years, as they drove to London each day. They worked on the buses and seemed to count each day they worked as a day nearer to their retirement. They spoke often of the day they could enjoy their lovely barge and just relax after a lifetime of hard work. But the security they believed the purchase of their mooring had brought them, simply didn't exist; there was no security for anyone in that marina. The residents seemed to creep around, trying not to attract the attention of the owners or inadvertently breach one of the numerous rules.

Ken was also being pressured into giving evidence by two other people who didn't have the courage to do it themselves.

These two people had known Robbie since his arrival on the river in 1988. He had worked for them many, many times for next to nothing and often nothing at all. Robbie welded boats, fixed engines and anything else they needed, often for nothing more than a cup of tea and a sandwich. These two people could spot a good heart at 300 paces. Such was my need to be accepted in this group, I allowed this to go on for years. They were Robbie's friends so they had to be important in my life too. Swallowing what I instinctively knew to be happening, I just kept smiling.

In 2003, their avarice, like a label on a cheap piece of clothing, had finally chafed on me enough and I made the decision to cut them out of my life. For years I felt guilty about this and even went to a Buddhist leader for guidance. The guidance was to chant, take the action I believed was right and then accept full responsibility for it. But I just wouldn't change my mind about my decision; the relief I felt at no longer having them in my life was something I didn't want to sacrifice.

During the years that followed I forced myself to recognize the good things in them, the way they had always cared for their animals and given time to their children. I had to do this for myself, to acknowledge that we all have the capacity for kindness and compassion just as we have the capacity for greed and ruthlessness. But what I couldn't do, was unable to do, was to be drawn back into their world again; it was just too bleak and hungry.

When Ken made his statement and decision to go to court for the prosecution, these two people accompanied him. He stayed long enough to give his brief evidence. He clearly didn't want to be there and left at about 11 am, as soon as he had given his statement. My case continued until 5 pm and these two people stayed until the end. I felt nothing about their actions; I already understood who they were, but they hurt Robbie that day and made him question his own judgment.

When we came home from court Robbie sat at his computer desk, head in hands, and went through the years as though watching a film for the second time, seeing the things he'd missed the first time around.

'If I'd still been doing the work for them, they'd never have done it,' he said, staring out the window at the river. We both knew this was true but he wasn't able to say that I had been right all those years earlier. I would have gladly been wrong just to stop him seeing his own kindness as something he'd given to the wrong people. As William Blake said, 'It is easier to forgive an enemy than to forgive a friend.'

## JULY 2009

**July 12**[th]    Mum died today in Yeovil Hospital. I found her a week ago in her chair, in a deep sleep. I eventually realised, when she didn't wake up even for another cigarette, that something was wrong. The hospital atoned for their torture of my dad by caring gently for my mum while she left this life. I always felt Mum would never see us marry.

When I was about eight o r n i n e I a s k e d my mum a question. 'Why does Dad have one job and you have two?'
She looked a bit puzzled and replied, 'I only have one job.'

'No you don't. You do people's cleaning and then you come home a n d  do the cooking and look after us and Dad.'

Mum had been awarded a scholarship while at school in Poplar but like many poor kids of that generation, she had been unable to take it up and had to leave school at thirteen to help bring in some money. Apart from her w o r k  i n  a munitions factory during the war, Mum had kept us alive by cleaning up other people's mess.

My question to her that day just seemed an ordinary one to a child. It was thirty years later that I was to hear the phrase, 'The personal is political,' while sitting in on a lecture at Nottingham University. I've never really known if I'm a feminist or even what feminism really means. But I feel it is something to do with mum's swollen knees and Dad

236

calling her in from the kitchen to change the channel on the television.

## SEPTEMBER 2009

**September 25<sup>th</sup>** Robbie answered the phone; it was the marina office. Detective Freeman and another officer wanted to speak to him. He left, telling me to hide the computers, but a few seconds later he walked back in followed by the detectives. They were going to arrest Robbie and confiscate our laptops.

'Have you come about my car?' I asked, knowing the answer. My car had been vandalised for the third time a couple of days earlier and I had reported it with that British air of acceptance that nothing would ever be done.

'I'm afraid not,' Detective Freeman said. 'It's about the dog.'
They could no longer do anything to me as I'd been sentenced and punished. Despite Veronica's barrister pushing for repeated prison sentences, one after the other, each time I refused to say where Hess was, Judge Simpton realised that my barrister would fight this.

'I'd take that to the High Court,' he assured me.

'He doesn't know where Hess is!' I pleaded, the first lie I'd told since this whole thing had started. Then the question I'd always wanted to ask.

'If I phone the police now and tell them that the person who has been looking after my dog for two months has refused to give it back, what would I be told?'

'You'd probably be told that it's a civil matter,' replied Detective Freeman.

'Then why have I been to prison and why are you arresting Robbie?'

'Someone with a lot more power than me has told us to do this,' he said. 'Judge Simpton wants Robbie arrested. He believes that the case wasn't dealt with properly in the beginning.'

But this didn't answer my question. What was it that Veronica had said during the first phone call to the police that made them treat this as a criminal matter and not a civil one? Clearly she didn't tell them that we had been caring for Hess for two months. But didn't they ask her any questions? How did Lin get the dog in the first place? Did she break into your boat? How long has she been looking after him? I often wonder if it was Veronica who actually called the police or was it someone else, someone whose name would register along the phone line? Why would a Crown Court Judge order the C.I.D. to arrest Robbie over a mongrel dog that I had already served a prison sentence for? No one will ever know and no one with influence will ever care enough to find out. And does it really matter anyway?

I didn't recognize, until much later, how brave this officer had been to say what he had said, acknowledging that something had been wrong with my case from the beginning; that it had been a civil case, relentlessly turned into a criminal one. Only his word, 'probably' held it back and kept him safe. It also explained something else; why the first part of my hearing in the Bridgewater Magistrates' Court had been spent discussing whether it was actually the right court for my case to be heard in. I didn't understand why they were discussing it; at this point I didn't realise that my case could be considered anything other than a crime.

What was clear was that these two men did not want to be doing this. They looked embarrassed and I felt embarrassed for them. Is this what they'd trained to do? Is this why they'd spent hours poring over books, taking exams, in order to chase a reckless, difficult woman who'd refused to return an old dog to whom she'd made a promise?

The less senior one then said, 'There must be something wrong if you were willing to go to prison for the dog.'

But nothing I said made any difference, that is until I asked, 'Do you know Stuart Redman?' Detective Freeman's head shot up. 'Stuart Redman, Head of Serious Crime?'

'He may be that now but he wasn't when Robbie and I knew him. We were the only people around here who would give a statement against 'Stev', Trevor Steel, after he broke into someone's boat and attacked Robbie's sister. She was lying next to their two year old son in bed. No one else would speak to him or give a statement, not even the people whose boat he broke in to. Just ask Stuart Redman about us.'

The boat Stev broke into was the one being rented by the same two people who encouraged Ken to give evidence against me. They were living in it until Stev was able to skipper their new boat around to Washford. They needed Stev, or believed they did, so they made the excuse which is an accepted part of our community.

'We don't bring the police into this sort of thing. We take care of it ourselves,' he told me, the day he came around trying to protect his partner from going to court to give evidence about the attack, while trying to keep Robbie on side at the same time. It was a difficult juggling act for him as Robbie loved his sister very much. Somehow Robbie got over their refusal to help have Stev prosecuted. He is much more forgiving than me. But their attitude to the role of the police in dealing with crime in our community had apparently changed by the time it came to the case of Hess.

The relationship between Stev and Robbie's sister was one that impacted on our lives for many years. He hated Robbie and threatened to kill him, accusing him of sleeping with his own sister. He was a damaged man who damaged others in turn. One night he stood outside our boat for hours, screaming abuse at Robbie, trying to get him to go outside. We called the police and waited for them to show up. A few hours after Stev left, they arrived.

Often Robbie's sister would turn up at our boat, moored across the pontoon to theirs, in the middle of the night, carrying a computer or some other piece of equipment that Stev had been trying to smash. Her need to keep these things safe seemed to override her need to keep herself safe. During this time Robbie was drinking heavily and this man and his death threats were always in his head.

Robbie's sister kept a shotgun on the boat; as farmers' children shotguns were a normal part of life. One day Robbie decided that we should try to remove it from their boat as Stev lived there and in the hands of someone who was threatening to kill him, it wasn't a good situation. I offered to go aboard to try to find it. After searching around for a while I was very pleased with myself when I found it hidden under the bunk. When I took it back to our boat Robbie found it quite funny that I didn't know the difference between a shotgun and an air rifle.

Finally Robbie persuaded his sister to give him the shotgun and boxes of cartridges. Our intention was to take it back to his parents' farm in Cornwall. But one night, after another flare up between Stev and Robbie's sister, Robbie got drunk and loaded the shotgun. I was in bed, trying to get some needed sleep for the next day's teaching, when I heard the first shot; it came from inside our boat. Robbie had fired the shotgun up through the deck. I lay in bed no knowing what to do. A drunken

241

Robbie is hard to reason with; a drunken and angry Robbie is volatile and completely unreachable. Then I heard another bang, louder than the first. I got up and went into the galley where Robbie was standing pointing the shotgun at the fridge freezer. He had fired through the door, shattering cartons of milk. Oddly, there appeared to be no 'exit wound' as they say in TV police dramas. It appeared as though the cartons of milk had stopped the bullet. Robbie then left the boat, carrying the shotgun, and I could hear him in the boatyard firing it off. My first thought was that if someone calls the police they'll come down and shoot this mad looking man. So I called his son and asked him to come down to try to calm his dad. But even though Robbie was doing this, there was a part of me that knew he hadn't completely lost control, that there was an element of pretence in his actions; this was Robbie's way of sending Stev a message.

Years earlier Robbie's Silesian mum told me that when the children were young she would save all her damaged crockery for the times when she needed to make a point; when her five children, her husband or the farm began to drive her mad. At these times she would smash all the chipped and cracked plates. With her family believing they were her best, she would dramatically throw the plates to the floor. When she did this the children would quieten down and her husband would realise that she had been pushed a bit too far. I believe that the shotgun incident was Robbie's version of smashing crockery.

Robbie finally came back to the boat and I could hear him mumbling to himself. When he eventually came to bed he brought the shotgun with him and placed it between us. I lay there pretending to be asleep but in my head I was thinking, 'I have to go to work in the morning, sit in a staffroom with normal people and talk about Ofsted. I have to sit and face thirty-two shiny little people and help them to make a replica of an Ancient Greek vase'

This part of the Stev story was something I didn't share with the detectives that day on our boat.

'We know you're not bad people,' the junior detective continued, 'but we've been told to do this and we don't have a choice.'

The detectives walked out of the boat with Robbie and our two laptops. On the laptops were emails linking us to Maria and Maria to Hess. I believe I then began sending texts to Maria, urgent texts, desperate texts.

'Move Hess now!!!'

'Robbie arrested. Move Hess now!!'

Forgetting that the police had warned us that they'd use any means, including surveillance, to find Hess, I sent these texts. I wanted to drive over to Maria's but feared that I'd be followed, so I spent the day waiting and chanting and talking, my stomach knotted and the tears waiting.

Several police officers we know, both retired and serving, have insisted that they simply don't do this kind of thing. One, who had recently retired from the force, told Robbie, 'We don't even spend this much time looking for a paedophile!'

He also offered to 'do some digging' for us to try to find out what was really going on. But fearing he would become embroiled in something, we declined his offer. It felt as though we had committed some offence that was far greater than the theft of a mongrel dog.

Robbie was released that night and came home putting on a good show of nonchalance. But he was angry towards me, cutting me off sharply when I spoke. He took charge of the situation and my thoughts had to be locked away. I knew that nothing I had to say would be of value or considered. Anything I said would make him angry, so I did what I had to do, iron his shirt, watched him pack his gear and went to his gig, just as I had for the past seventeen years.

**September 26**th The band had a gig at The Barge in Honiton. At the end Robbie made a big thing over the microphone about having spent all of yesterday in a police cell. He sounded proud, almost showing off. He gave a quick run through of the Hess story, to the small and reasonably disinterested audience. There was some mottled applause. Then the band packed up the gear and we went to the kebab shop to do some more work on our greasy and early death. Everything seemed normal, or as normal as it ever can be with our lives.

**September 27**<sup>th</sup> Robbie is angry. He shouts at everything I say, or suggest, or mention. He tells me to go stay at my sister's for a week. I go to a Buddhist meeting but call him when I pull up outside. Mistake. We speak of Maria and Hess then he says, 'Which phone are you using?' and hangs up when we realise what we've done. Would they really bug our mobiles? We suspected they'd bugged our landline when a familiar sound of recording came on the line one day in June, shortly after Robbie had been asked to go to the police station. I recognised the clicking sound from the prison phones that recorded all conversations. We told no one, too certain that we wouldn't be believed and worse still, be thought of as nutcases. Why would they spend the time and money bugging a phone over a ten year old mongrel dog, a dog for which I'd served a prison sentence? We'd grown tired of the looks people gave us when we voiced our suspicions that there was something underhanded about our situation; there couldn't be, not in Great Britain. Things like that simply don't happen in a civilised country. Robbie was less reticent than I and spoke openly, but I was the one considered insane so I kept quiet and let Robbie speak for me.

I went back to the boatyard to find Robbie. He was by his workshop. I rolled down the window.

'Where's your phone?' he said.
His face was rigid. I knew the look. He snatched the phone out of my hand, took out the SIM card and put in a 'Pay As You Go' one that we kept as a spare.

245

'Go to your sister's! Don't come back for a week!'

I we*nt to Amelia and Stephen's boat and seemed to* cry for hours. Later I was to feel great shame for this when I learned that Amelia had only just been given a diagnosis of breast and bone cancer. She said nothing about it to me; she simply kept filling me with cups of hot, sweet tea.

At this time Robbie was searching for me, cycling around Washford, believing, I was later to learn, that I had gone to Maria's, even though he'd disabled my car to stop me doing so. He arrived at Amelia and Stephen's, sweat running down his face and, with near hysteria, shouted, 'Do you trust me? Do you trust me?' I nodded, afraid of his anger and his fear. Then he left, telling me he'd disabled my car but he would now put that right and I was to go to my sister's. I cried again. What was happening?

I went to Bobby and Nig's in Frome, after asking them if I could stay for a few days. I am blessed with friends like these. We chanted and did Gongyo.


**September 28**[th] I will write the ending today. Robbie and I were to go to Williton Registry Office at 11 am to register our forthcoming marriage at Taplow Court. I phoned Robbie to ask him what I should do.

'Book it for another day. I have something to do this morning and then I'll be over to see you.'
I was relieved. He was no longer angry with me and I felt safe. Robbie loved me still and that was all that

mattered. I had always wondered why he was with me but felt so grateful that he was.

I was sitting on the couch stroking Bobby and Nig's dogs when Robbie arrived on his FJ1200, the bike on which we'd spent so many hours. I let him in but kept standing; so did he. He didn't look at me as he said,

'I've taken Hess back.'

There is a space, a time, just before an earthquake, when all goes still and the birds stop singing. Then the buildings fall, crushing the life we know.

The floor seemed to fall away and I began to shake. I looked at him but didn't see Robbie. Who was this man? What had the past two years, or seventeen, been about?

The first words I spoke were to my sister-in-law, who was making the wedding invitations for us. I dialled her number.

'Can you stop making the invitations; the wedding is off. Robbie has taken Hess back.'

To me there seemed to be no need to say any more than this. I believed my bottom line had always been written in the sky for everyone to see. Robbie had simply not looked up to see the trails of white in the blue.

'Are you sure?' he asked, with a look that the word 'stricken' was intended for.

'There's no way back from this,' I said and he left.

I was still standing by the couch in the room I knew so well but everything looked unfamiliar, the clothes I was wearing, the walls, my life for the past seventeen years. Who was the man who had just walked out the door, the man who once screamed at me in frustration, 'What do you want!? What do you want!?'

'I want to know you're always on my side,' I said, 'just like I'm always on yours.'

I called Maria. How did Robbie manage to get Hess away from her? She had looked after him for two years and I knew that she loved him just as much as she did her two other dogs. What was happening? What had Robbie said that could have made her do this?

## MARIA'S STORY

*Hess wasn't with me when Robbie came to see me. He'd phoned to say that he needed to come over to see me. In my head I was thinking, 'Why?' I knew it was about Hess as I'd moved him to Janice's two days earlier after receiving Lin's texts to say that Robbie had been arrested. Robbie sounded panicked on the phone so I said, 'What's this all about?'*

*'Can't talk on the phone; the walls have ears,' he replied.*

*He arrived in the dark, alone on his motorbike. He seemed really on edge, checking behind him and looking around the garden.*

*'Can anyone get in your garden?' he asked.*

248

'No, why would they?' I said.

Inside I thought that this was quite bizarre behaviour. I kept thinking, 'This is so over the top,' but still didn't know why he was here. What I thought was also quite odd was that he was alone. Robbie and Lin were practically joined at the hip and I remember thinking, 'Where's Lin? Why isn't she with him?'

I made him a coffee and then asked him what it was all about.

'I've been arrested and they took our laptops for forensic analysis.'

'Forensic analysis!' I said. 'What do you think this is, CSI? Robbie, let's get this into perspective; this is a ten year old mongrel. Are you seriously trying to tell me that the Somerset police have those kinds of resources because I'm bloody sure our police don't?'

Robbie looked straight at me and said, 'Maria, these people are deadly serious. They have the power to do personal surveillance and have every intention of doing so. Your contact details are on both our computers. It won't take them long to arrive at your door.'

Robbie stopped talking for a second and looked at me, moving himself back in his seat. He then said, 'That bastard Judge will throw away the key! And trust me Maria you will not survive in prison. '

I didn't make eye contact with him. I continued with the ironing I had been doing when he arrived but in my head I was thinking, 'Shit, this man is serious.'

Robbie kept emphasising that I would definitely go to prison.

'You'll lose everything Maria, your good name, your business, your dogs, everything.'

'I'll just tell them he's dead and I'll produce ashes,' I said.

'They'll forensically test them,' he replied.

'How will they be able to tell that it's not Hess? They'll be the ashes of a dog,' I said.

Robbie then said, 'They'll test them for age and breed.'

'Oh Robbie, get a life! Are you seriously, seriously trying to tell me that the Somerset police have those resources to spend on a ten year old mongrel?'

'The bottom line Maria is they have every intention of coming here and arresting you,' he said. 'They're that close,' and gestured the two inches that they were away from arresting me.

Robbie said that he'd used his motorbike to come over because they had his van and Lin's car under surveillance. He also said that he'd gone to another area first to throw them off the scent in case they were following him.

Robbie then began to tell me that there were other things on his laptop, relating to his [2]income tax, that he needed to keep quiet.

'So what do you want from me Robbie?'

'The only way to stop this is to give the dog back. I've had assurances from the copper who arrested me that if the dog is returned this will all be dropped.'

*I kept ironing, saying nothing. I just kept thinking, 'I can't do this. I can't give him back to a life of hell. I just can't.'*

*I'd had Hess for two years. When Lin brought him to me in August 2007 I'd just lost my golden Labrador, Seamus, and I'd just taken on another rescue. I remember asking, when I first received the phone call from Lin, what breed Hess was and she told me that he was a Lurcher/Great Dane cross. I told Lin that I would foster him on condition that it didn't upset my rescue dog as she had been sold via the internet three times and had been shut up in a flat. The first nine months of her life had been hell and I was trying to settle her.*

*When Lin first arrived with Hess I realised that my vision of a huge dog was unfounded; he was about the size of a greyhound but with a larger build and he had the eyes of Seamus, a Labrador's eyes. I made Lin a cup of tea and Hess stuck to her like glue. I remember thinking, 'This dog adores her.'*

*Lin was crying as she gave me some background about how she'd acquired Hess. She told me that Hess' given name was 'Jesus', pronounced the Spanish way, but Veronica was the only person who called him this; everyone knew him as Hess. Lin then said that Veronica had told the police she had stolen the dog. She felt that the case may be dropped as everyone knew she hadn't stolen him but had been caring for him for a long time. Lin said that when she left me she was going straight to the police station to talk to them.*

When Lin left, Hess sat at the street door with his nose pressed up against it. He cried and he sat there for fifteen to twenty minutes. I got a biscuit for him. I got one of my dog's toys. Nothing would get him away from the door. All of a sudden he took himself upstairs and he sat by the window looking out. I went up and stood at the bedroom door and said, 'Come on Hess. Come downstairs and join us. She won't be long. She's not going to leave you.'

I came back down but he stayed upstairs and about twenty minutes later he appeared at the living room door. He came over to me and sat by the side of me. I leant forward and I said, 'Don't worry. I'll look after you until she comes back.' Then my rescue dog picked up one of her toys and dropped it in front of him. He lifted his head back and I put my arm around him and cuddled him then he went on the dog bed and my rescue took every toy out of the box and took them over to him. She sat on the end of the bed with him and he finally put his head down and went to sleep, with my rescue dog cuddled up beside him.

He was stressed because Lin had gone and she was obviously the focal point for him. When I took him for a walk I wouldn't let him off the lead because I didn't know what he would do. After three days I could see that both Hess and my rescue dog were desperate to play so I let him off. They ran around together for ages and had a great time. Hess was really enjoying himself and was so well behaved. Hess and my rescue became inseparable.

252

One day, a couple of weeks after Hess had arrived; I was stroking his ears when he let out a loud yelp. It made me jump and I initially thought I'd hurt him but didn't know how, as I was being quite gentle. I then thought that he may have a problem with his ears so I checked them for the smell of canker and then I cleaned them out. Hess sat quietly while I did this.

A couple of weeks later he was sitting in the back of my car after a walk. I ruffled my dog's ears and kissed her. As I went to do the same with Hess he screamed. It put me on edge and I was very careful about how I touched him after that, always making sure I was visible as I approached him and I always let him know when I was going to touch him. The next time Lin came to visit him I asked her about it. She then told me that she had experienced the same thing and, although she couldn't prove it, thought that he'd been rough handled by Veronica when she was drunk. It was at this point that I also asked Lin if he had a problem with water because whenever I filled the water bowls up Hess would watch me, following me to the tap and following me back, watching me put the bowl down. He then always drank from it but not excessively. If I filled all three bowls he would drink from all three. I've had rescue dogs for 35 years and I've never seen this type of behaviour in a dog before. He obviously had a thing about water. However, by the time he left me he had no problem with water. He always knew that water was readily available, even on our walks.

*After I had had Hess for a while he grew confident, relaxed and at ease, which was why it was such a shock when I inadvertently went to step over him some five months after he'd come to stay. He was in a deep sleep. I quietly said, 'Come on Hess, move. I want to get by.' He screamed, leapt up and pinned himself against the couch shaking. At that point I knew for sure. Everything fell into place. This dog was constantly on edge, never knowing when he was going to be kicked or hit or shouted at. This dog was used to being terrified.*

*As I stood ironing that Sunday night I watched as Robbie became more stressed and paranoid. I waited for the police to knock on the door.*

*'If you let me take him back I promise you I will not let this rest. Give it a few weeks and I'll go and get him back. I promise you he will not stay with her. I promise you, he will not stay. Four weeks max, I'll leave him there for four weeks then I'll get him back. It won't be any longer. I've already been over there and checked it out. It's an end bungalow with a field at the back. I'll pick my moment and grab him.'*

*'But if this is as bad as you're telling me Robbie, I'll never be able to have him back.'*

*'No, I'll find a good home for him, one where he'll never be found. You'll just have to trust that I've done that.'*

*I knew he meant what he was saying. I knew his intention was to get Hess back again but his desperation was palpable. I made him promise that*
254

he would keep his word and get Hess back, not for me but for Hess, and that he would find him a good home where he could live out his days in peace. I said, 'Right Robbie, you need to do this before I change my mind; tomorrow morning.'

'Yes,' he said, 'the sooner the better. The police will be here at any moment.'

We made arrangements for him to pick up Hess at 10'clock the following morning and he left. At some point that night Robbie had told me that Lin didn't know he was here. What he failed to tell me was that she didn't know what he was intending to do.

I didn't sleep that night. I kept going over and over it in my head. I had taken Hess over to Janice's two days earlier, just in case the police arrived, and I knew that Janice would be walking Hess along with her dogs about 6 o'clock in the morning before she went to work. I went to where I knew she would be with Hess and her dogs. Our dogs spotted each other and ran towards each other like star struck lovers. I'd texted Janice to tell her that I'd be picking up Hess but didn't tell her why. Hess was all over me. We were all together again, the pack. I walked up to Janice. We were both crying. I told her what was happening but she already instinctively knew that Hess was going.

I brought him back, gave him breakfast and had already booked him an appointment at the vets to get his anal glands done. I knew Veronica wouldn't bother and I wanted to give him as much time in comfort as I could. I was crying so much at the vets that the practice

255

manager came over and spoke to me. I told her in brief what was happening and she cried too. The nurse who did his treatment was in tears.

On the way back home I met Penny, my neighbour. She asked why I was crying and I told her. She came in to say goodbye to him and to tell me that she knew someone who could 'lose' him for me. Even at that late stage we were thinking we could hide him. But Robbie had convinced me that the police would be knocking at my door if they didn't get Hess back. I then took all the dogs out for their last walk together. We came back. I packed up all his food and put his new collar on him. I got his new lead and his favourite toy and then my phone rang. It was Robbie.

Robbie didn't want to come to my house as he thought someone was following him so he asked me to meet him on a side road. I walked Hess to the place and sat on the pavement with my arms around him, talking to him, telling him that I would always love him, that this was his home and that this would always be his home, no matter how long it took. He was leaning against me. And as if he knew, he nuzzled his head in my shoulder and kept nuzzling my hand to stroke him. Then a beaten up white car pulled up with Robbie in it. He got out and he said, 'Hello Maria. I've had to borrow this car because the police know my van.' He then took the lead and I bent down and cuddled Hess, gave him a kiss and said, 'Bye baby boy, see you soon.'

*Robbie put Hess in the back of the car and as he drove off Hess was looking out of the back window at me with an expression that said, 'Why are you doing this to me? What have I done?'*

*I sat on the pavement and sobbed as people walked past. I will take that look to my grave and one of my prayers every night is that he'll forgive me. It would have been better if he'd died because at least he would have been in God's hands. Now I just don't know where he is. Is he being cared for? Is someone loving him? I dream about him and in my dream he's back with me, right here.*

*A couple of hours later my phone rang. It was Lin. She was distraught, wanting to know why I'd given him back. I thought she knew and then it dawned on me; Robbie hadn't told her what he was going to do.*

*'I didn't know. If I'd have known I would have come over and taken him,' she sobbed.*

*I replied, 'And then what Lin, then what?'*

## SEPTEMBER 28th – NOVEMBER 5th 2009

I remember sleeping on a couch at Chris and Katy's house in London. The couch was covered in a stone coloured fabric. It had tiny cat paw prints running along the arm, where one of their three cats had walked through Chris' oil paints on a day he'd set aside for creativity. The pattern added interest to an otherwise ordinary couch. I slept on this couch in the front room of their large Victorian house. They closed the ceiling-high pine doors which separated this room

257

from the adjoining one. They gave me the room in which I would begin my grieving. I slept and woke at 4 am each morning. Grief is delayed when we wake. It has a cruel way of allowing us those seconds in the gentle place, the place before. And then the pain comes.

I remember walking Bob, the warm part of my life, each day, twice, down to the small green and around the place they call 'The Meadow'. I remember an arrangement in October. Mum's ashes, along with Dad's, which had now been retrieved from under the flagstone in Mum's garden, were to be scattered at Stolford. I didn't go. It meant nothing.

My grief was a mixture of colours; the loss of Robbie, the pain of Hess, my mum. The colours swirled and I was unable to tell one from the other.

I remember going to a wedding with happy people. I remember this.

I arranged to meet Robbie at Washford Common. Sometimes we walked Bob there and wondered about the fresh flowers that s o m e o n e  had been taping to the fence for years. A lost love? Perhaps this would be me now. Something was brittle and frozen between us. I hugged him with the hope of finding him but there was only hardness now, his arms stiff and dutiful, like a soldier. Where had we gone?

I tried to glue us back together for a few months. We had cursory sex and cursory conversations. During this time I fought to make what Robbie had done, small and insignificant. He told

258

himself and those who would listen, that he had taken that action to stop Maria going to prison. This was a small truth. The big truth was that he was afraid. But I had to preserve the man others had constructed out of broken engines and rock music, the man who looked as though he could fight the world and win. But the shadow between us stayed. It sat down with us when we ate. It travelled with us wherever we went and when we laid down in bed it was there in the space between us. I still made plans for us, but Robbie had already left; just his life remained, walking around, keeping busy.

Many months later I was to learn that the morning Robbie had returned Hess, he had gone to the marina cafe for a cup of tea. Tess was there and Robbie said to her, 'I have to do two things today, keep Maria out of prison and save my relationship with Lin.' By the time Tess told me this it was too late, too late to tell him that I understood just what it had done to him to take Hess back.


### MAY 2010

**May 1st 2010** Robbie and I split up today. I couldn't say it. I couldn't say that what he did was right. How could I lie to the man I loved so much, the man I'd never lied to in our seventeen years together? So he raged and cried and held his head in his hands but still I couldn't say it.

'I believe you did what you thought was right.' I gave him this much. But it wasn't enough. I felt him slipping away but I couldn't say the words that would keep him. And even if I had been able to say them, it would never have been enough; Robbie knew the truth and no needy, desperate lie of mine could change that.

**These things I miss** The private word games that locked us in and others out, the full moons on the river, the early morning debates, the late night homecomings along frozen pontoons, the 100mph bike rides tucked behind his right shoulder, the fast kisses half out the door, the charity shop love I found for him in loud shirts and ankle-hugging jeans, the raw turnip left on the plate.

### 3$^{rd}$ week of May 2010

Robbie is with someone else now; I believe the foundations were being prepared for a while.

### February 18$^{th}$ 2011

Today I swam in One Moon Bay in Southern Thailand. I was with my two sons, Big John and all of my grandchildren, the people I worry about so much. We are here for Chris and Katy's wedding. As I floated in the Andaman Sea, I concentrated on living in the moment. I have been trying to do this and it helps. The moment has no memory.

When I returned to the villa there was a text on my phone from Tess; it said, 'Veronica died today'.

I felt sad but sadness comes in so many forms. I was sad that anyone should die that way, eaten alive, like the zebra in 'Life of Pi'. I was sad that the hole in her life was so huge she needed to fill it with alcohol. I was sad that I never got to know who she really was, that I never tried hard enough to find out, that I allowed my fear of her bitterness to stop me looking for the real person beneath. But my first thought when I read Tess' text was, 'I wonder where Hess is. I hope someone is loving him.'

### 2012

*When my son John stopped drinking, he joined a group for recovering alcoholics. It wasn't AA, as there was something in the AA method that didn't reach him. But it was a group in which, like AA, the sharing of experiences was a large part in the recovery.*

*One day he told me a story that someone had shared. This person drank all day, every day. He shook so much when he woke up that he kept a bottle of something next to his bed so that it was the first thing he reached for in the morning. Often he had no money with which to buy the bottle and some mornings he vomited before he had time to drink. So he devised a plan. Next to his bed he began to keep a pair of sheer tights and when he woke up he vomited into them; what came through the mesh had enough alcohol in it to keep him going, so he drank it.*

261

For the first thirteen years that Robbie and I were together, alcohol was the oil in his machine. When he realized, and admitted to himself, that his drinking was out of control he tried different things, strategies that would still allow him to drink. One of his plans was to drink only beer and not the Irish whiskey and red wine. He found himself drinking as much beer as it took to make up for the alcohol he had given up. He then decided to drink only at weekends but drank enough from Friday night until late Sunday night to make up for the missing five days.

One day, after fighting with his youngest son in the street, Robbie stopped drinking. No 'steps', no 'sharing', he just stopped. Robbie is clever with words and has a way of cutting through and getting to the core. He said that alcoholism, like any addiction, is about chasing the good times we had when we were high and hoping to re-create them once more.

Use of the 'addiction' metaphor to describe my time with Robbie isn't precise but it is as close as I can get. It was always enough for me that I was in his company, breathing the same air, waiting for the smile or the word, a mention of my name in his conversation.

When he wasn't around, it was as though a part of my life was suspended, waiting for his return.

A few months after we made the decision to separate, I asked him to meet me at Riverview Country Park, the place I walked Bob, the place where I could look across the Washford River to the village and the past twenty years of my life. I had written down what I *wanted to say to him because I knew I would cry a lot and not be able to get the words out. This behaviour has always angered Robbie and his anger had always scared me. With anger he could force my words back down my throat where I would leave them, burning away like acid.*

*I climbed into his van, shaking so hard that the words were a blur on the page. And I told him this:*

**'I'm so sorry I didn't see or understand how painful it must have been for you to return Hess. It took a different kind of courage to do that, knowing what you were risking, and my reaction, what you could lose. I'm so sorry that I didn't see it. But I do now. Be it 6 months, 6 years or 6 lifetimes, I want a future with you. You're in my heart. I tried to be angry; I was. I tried to be strong; I was. But I woke up on Monday July 5th and my heart had opened and inside it, there you were. I didn't want another day to go by without telling you. I'm scared of the pain. I didn't know I could hurt so much. But I knew that if I didn't tell you, I'd regret it for the rest of my life. I'm so sorry. What I did in going to prison was the easy part; what you did took a kind of courage I didn't have. I'm not saying I've changed, that life will always be calm. We're both passionate about life and the world around us so that doesn't equal a calm life. But I can now see how my actions and lack of wisdom can impact and hurt others. I have**

*to do this and I have to tell you because I don't want you to live with the pain and burden of something I have caused. You're a good man and I want you to be happy.'*

*I left Robbie sitting silent in the van and drove away. Four days later, a three page, single-spaced letter arrived. It was attached to an email which said, 'Read! Print! Keep!' The exclamations marks are his.*

*Robbie had always told me that he fell in love with my mind, the way I see the world in an odd way. His letter told me it was my mind he had fallen out of love with; the one part of me I can't amend, the part of me that had splintered under the weight of my need to keep him. It was my mind, he wrote, that had destroyed us and would destroy any other relationship I may have.*

*Who could I phone but Flick? Fifteen years earlier it had been Flick I phoned when Robbie told me he'd slept with someone else while in Cornwall with his band. And it was Flick who told me,*

*'Do what **you** want to do; not what other people think you should do.'*

*So I stayed with him, made it right in my head, knowing, always knowing, that there was nothing Robbie could ever do that would make me leave him.*

*It was 6 am and Flick was silent as I read to her each bitter word. And she was in my corner, as always, holding the bloodied sponge, trying to stem the flow. My best friend. After Robbie and I broke up it was always Flick I called, sobbing, when I found a*

264

*part of my life with him, hiding in the lights across the river or in the dusty corners of a remembered song.*

*I considered including Robbie's letter in this book. The reason I didn't is because I believe it was the first letter, the one into which we throw our grief and anger and relief and regret; the one we burn before we sit back down to write the second letter, the one that comes from the ashes of the first.*

*Whether we believe addiction is an illness or a chosen behaviour is of no importance to me. I choose to use the word 'recovery' simply because this is how it feels. I believed my love for Robbie to be a terminal illness. My words to him that day were the mesh through which I was vomiting, hoping once more to reach the man to whom I had been addicted for seventeen years.*

*I don't know if there is a difference between love and addiction and I have no interest in wading through the myriad of books, written mainly for women, which may help me know; as if learning this difference will somehow melt away the pain.*

*All I know is this: after our break-up, my hand would inadvertently go across my heart when I spoke of him, as though I was trying to save those tiny pieces, lost in the weave of our life. The day I stopped doing this was the day I knew my recovery had begun.*

This is a true story and all events happened as recounted. Some names and locations have been changed.

# Notes

1. *I doubted Sophie's story and thought perhaps she and her husband had been smuggling drugs. When I was released I emailed Sophie and asked if she would let me see her court papers. She sent them to me. The papers said that the case involved the 'fraudulent evasion of excise duty'...*

2. *In 2004, Robbie's work van was broken in to, the back window removed and all his work tools stolen. Robbie called the police and an officer came out. He asked Robbie whether he had knocked on any doors to find out if anyone knew anything. Robbie replied, 'I thought that was your job.' Robbie's tools are not only specialist but vital to him being able to make a living, so using the £2,000 he had managed to save for his next tax bill to buy replacements was an option. A few days after the robbery, a small package addressed to Robbie arrived from the Bridgewater police. It contained a 'Do It Yourself' fingerprint kit. At that point, Robbie made the decision not to pay his tax bill.*

# References

*A Mighty Heart – Mariane Pearl'. Published by Virago 2001*

*The Complete Works of Shakespeare – The Alexander Text. Published by Collins 1951*

*The Major Writings of Nichiren Daishonin – Volume one. Published by Soka Gakkai 1999*

*The Buddha, Geoff and Me – Edward Canfor-Dumas. Published by Rider 2005*

Lightning Source UK Ltd.
Milton Keynes UK
UKHW041827131118
332284UK00001B/213/P